THE WEYMOUTH HARBOUR TRAMWAY

THE WEYMOUTH HARBOUR TRAMWAY

J. H. LUCKING

OXFORD PUBLISHING CO.

ISBN 0-86093-304-0

Typesetting by:
Colin Powell Typesetting & Design, Bournemouth, Dorset

Printed in Great Britain by:
Biddles Ltd., Guildford and Kings Lynn

Published by:
Oxford Publishing Co.
Link House
West Street
POOLE, Dorset

British Library Cataloguing in Publication Data

Lucking, J. H.
The Weymouth harbour tramway. –(Branch line histories)
1. Street-railroads – England – Weymouth (Dorset) – History
I. Title II. Series
388.4'6'0942335 HE4719.W4

SOURCES AND ACKNOWLEDGMENTS

This book is based largely on original records, notably the following: tramway agreements, by courtesy of the Chief Executive, Borough of Weymouth & Portland; former BTHR files pertaining to the W&PR and the tramway, now in the Public Record Office, Kew; relevant files of the Board of Trade, also at Kew; deposited plans (Dorset County Record Office); Weymouth municipal records (Weymouth Local History Museum and Weymouth Harbour Master's office); and the files of two local newspapers, the *Dorset County Chronicle* and *The Southern Times*. The assistance of the several custodians and their staffs is gratefully acknowledged, with individual thanks to Mrs Betty Adams (Harbour Master's office), and Messrs. John Bligh (Weymouth Museum), Stuart Morris (Borough Engineer's department) and Geoffrey Pritchard (Chief Executive's department); also to Mr D.W. Munday, of the Railway Inspectorate, Department of Transport.

Special thanks are due to Mr David Wroe, of the Area Civil Engineer's office, BR, Bournemouth, for expert advice and for allowing me to consult plans and other official material; Mr Jack Vines, lately of the Station Master's office, Weymouth, for lending me the old station register quoted in Appendix II; and Mrs Maureen Attwooll, of Weymouth Reference Library, for drawing my attention to a number of items that I might otherwise have missed.

In 1954, on taking up an appointment on the quay, I began a close personal acquaintance with the tramway, and in writing about the events of the past thirty years have been able to draw extensively on my own notes. During that time I have also had the pleasure of knowing many of the railwaymen concerned. Their readiness to provide information has always been appreciated. I thank in particular Messrs. Ronald Copp, Brian Hook and Maurice Kent, and Sgt. Keith Fleetwood and Insp. Alcwyn Jones of the Transport Police. Mr David Vogt, Sealink Shipping Manager at Weymouth, and his assistant, Mr Michael Morgan, have also been most helpful. Lastly I thank my son, for scrutinising the manuscript, my wife, for cheerfully enduring all that writing a book entails, and my friend Colin Caddy, who cut the first sod – the initial suggestion that I should write the book was his. Illustrations are acknowledged individually where appropriate; the rest are my own.

CONTENTS

INTRODUCTORY NOTE

To the uninformed majority, the Channel Islands boat train painfully picking its way through today's summer traffic is simply a nuisance — at best a curiosity; but those who care for such things are aware that this unique sight is a last link with the time when Weymouth was a flourishing railway port. For seventy years and more the principal user of Weymouth harbour was the Great Western Railway, and almost the whole of the company's steamer traffic there, amounting to thousands of tons of goods and thousands of passengers annually, was conveyed through the town over the harbour tramway. Much of the tramway's former importance was maintained well into nationalisation. From about the mid-1950s, however, the changing pattern of transport resulted in a gradual decline until 1972, when the withdrawal of all Weymouth's railborne freight cast doubts over the line's continuing survival.

Not quite a branch line, nor yet just a siding, with many peculiarities and its own rule book, the Weymouth tramway offers the student of railways abundant interest, particularly if his preference is for the unusual. Its history is inseparably bound up with that of the quay itself, and the account that follows aims to cover both. Similarly, in selecting the illustrations, the aim has been not only to depict as many aspects of the tramway as possible, at different periods, but to compile at least some record of the traffic that has gone — of the years when the harbour trade was a major factor in Weymouth's economy, and the tramway was 'all part of it'.

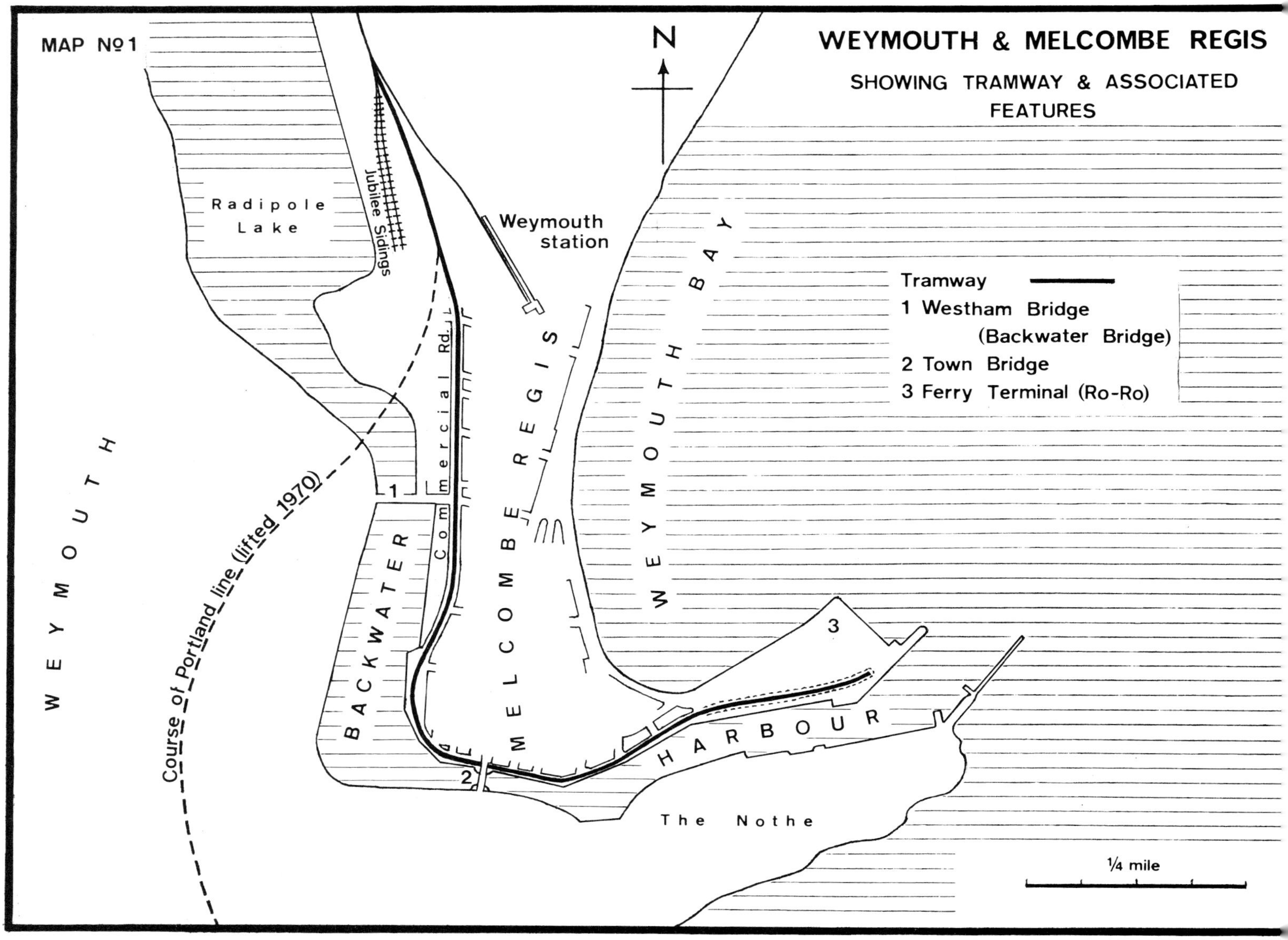

What has long been conveniently referred to as Weymouth embraces the once separate boroughs of Weymouth and Melcombe Regis. The railway in Weymouth lies in what is, strictly speaking, Melcombe Regis – i.e., to the north and east of the Harbour and Backwater. As will be seen, the tramway runs along the Melcombe Regis side of the water.

CHAPTER ONE
Origins

The coming of the railways affected many small ports adversely, the resulting decline in coastal shipping depriving them of much of their trade. Weymouth, on the other hand, was one that benefited. The particular circumstance that distinguished Weymouth was that in 1794 it had been designated by the Post Office as the packet station for the Channel Islands mails, the mail packets providing the first regular sailings between England and the islands. In 1845, for want of a Weymouth railway, the packet service was discontinued, but once the line was open (1857) Channel Islands sailings were restarted, with railway backing — a new enterprise on old foundations. The harbour tramway followed, though not immediately, to be followed in turn by other developments to meet the needs of the steamers. Increasingly Weymouth became a railway port and increasingly, as former trade disappeared, it was the cross-channel traffic — and the tramway — that kept the port alive.

The railway steamer service owed much, if not its very existence, to the Government packets. To make a comparable claim for the tramway would be an exaggeration, but the earliest proposal for a railway to the harbour does, in fact, date back to the time of the packets. In 1836 a Parliamentary Bill was deposited for a line to run from the Great Western Railway near Bath via Wincanton, Cerne Abbas and Dorchester, the Bath & Weymouth Great Western Union Railway. Weymouth Town Council, concerned not merely as local authority but, particularly, as harbour authority, assented to the proposal provided that the line was 'carried to the westward of the public Wharfs and Quays in the Backwater' — i.e., along the water's edge on the Melcombe Regis side of the harbour — and in April 1837 decided to petition the House of Commons in favour of the Bill. James Agnew Stevens, Post Office packet agent at Weymouth, recognised the railway's potential in connection with cross-channel traffic and foresaw the line's completion as leading to the 'considerable enlargement' of the harbour. At that early date, however, the Great Western itself had barely been started and in the event the Bill was withdrawn.

By now the wave of enthusiasm for railways that had marked the previous couple of years was subsiding, and another seven years elapsed before the question of a line to Weymouth was raised again. In 1844 Bills were deposited for two lines, one a branch from the Great Western near Corsham, the Wilts, Somerset & Weymouth Railway, and the other a westward extension of the London & South Western, the Southampton & Dorchester Railway. Both companies were incorporated in 1845, the former on 30th June and the latter on 21st July, and both Acts provided for a junction at Dorchester whereby S&D trains would have access to Weymouth over the WS&W. There was, however, no provision for a line to the harbour.

In the following Parliamentary session both companies sought to remedy that shortcoming, the WS&W by extending their authorised line and the S&D by means of a branch from Moreton, to give access to Weymouth, including the harbour, independently of the WS&W. Yet a third proposal for a harbour line was included in plans deposited for a westward continuation of the S&D, intended to link both Dorchester and Weymouth with Exeter and to be known as the Exeter, Dorchester, Weymouth Junction Coast Railway.

The Exeter line being dropped and the S&D's Weymouth branch held over to the following year, the field was left clear for the WS&W extension. This was unopposed and, with various other amendments to the original Act, was authorised on 3rd August 1846, from 'a certain Point in the Park in the Parish of Melcombe Regis . . . and terminating at or on the Quays . . . of Melcombe Regis'.

Since the WS&W was to conform to the 7ft. gauge of the Great Western while the S&D was to be 'narrow' — i.e., standard-gauge, exercise of the latter's running powers between Dorchester and Weymouth required the gauge to be mixed between those points, and the 1846 Act extended that provision to the harbour line, Section 18 stipulating that narrow gauge should be added to the broad 'if and when the Board of Trade shall deem the same to be convenient and desirable'.

To no avail: like the limited 'mania' of the mid-thirties the Railway Mania of the mid-forties was followed by a sharp downturn. With capital almost impossible to raise, construction of the WS&W itself dragged on for a further ten years, the original Parliamentary powers being twice renewed, and powers for the harbour extension were allowed to lapse.

The delay in completion was endured by those affected with much irritation and impatience, not least with regard to the harbour trade vis-a-vis Weymouth's ancient rival, Poole. Strange, then, that meeting on 24th December 1856, when the opening of the Weymouth line was at last in sight, the council resolved '. . . to write to the Secretary of the Great Western Railway Company that the Town Council of Weymouth will be most happy to render every assistance in their power to facilitate the conveyance of goods etc., from the Quays to the Railroad station, *except having any Tramroad in front of the Esplanade or in the Public Streets*'. What lay behind that proviso we shall never know, and what the Great Western were supposed to make of it is hard to guess, since a tramway was the only 'assistance' worth considering and previous proposals had enjoyed ready council support. The line to Weymouth was opened in January 1857. When the new steamer service started, the following April, it was without the benefit of rail connection to the quay.

This situation was obviously unsatisfactory but the Great Western, perhaps because it had only a minority interest in the steamers (12½ per cent of the authorised capital of the company operating them, the Weymouth & Channel Islands Steam Packet Company) and certainly through a reluctance to add to an already considerable outlay on the Weymouth line, showed no inclination to improve it. It was left to a director of the Packet Company, James Aldridge Devenish, to take the initiative. Writing to the Great Western in March 1861, he offered to lay before them what he called 'a well digested scheme for the completion of a tramway'. He proposed to form a company, with a capital of £10,000 in £10 shares, for the express purpose of linking the harbour to the station. The preamble to a draft prospectus reads:

> On the completion of the Railways, or concurrently, it was always intended to form a Tramway from the stations to the Harbour as in other Seaport Towns, although greatly needed this has not been done, it is submitted in consequence hitherto neither the Town or Railways have derived the full advantage of the two lines being opened to Weymouth.

The estimated cost of 'making a Tramway from the Railway Station to the Steam Packet Station and Pier' was about £5,000, made up as follows:

	£	s.	d.
Rails	420	0	0
Bolts and Fastenings	120	0	0
Laying in Point and Crossing Quay Works	400	0	0
Timber for Road	840	0	0
Tunnel under Bridge	700	0	0
Laying Road and Repairs to Wall along Commercial Road	500	0	0
Timber Viaduct from the Foundry to Ferry's Yard	800	0	0
Engineering and Superintendence	250	0	0
Parliamentary and Law Expenses	500	0	0
Contingencies	300	0	0
Total by Viaduct	4830	0	0
Stone Wall instead of Viaduct add	750	0	0
	5580	0	0

Devenish intended his tramway to be a toll road, over which the Great Western would have worked the traffic at its own expense, though at a considerable saving on the cost of road cartage. This was given as £1,162.10s.0d. per annum — 15,500 tons at 1s.6d. (7½p) per ton. The cost by tramway was estimated as £645.16s.8d., or not much more than half, made up of 6d. (2½p) per ton for locomotive power (£387.10s.0d.) and a suggested toll of 4d. (1½p) per ton (£258.6s.8d.). Tolls, it seems, were expected to do no more than cover the £250.0s.0d. quoted as interest on the cost of construction, leaving unresolved such questions as liability for maintenance; but it is probable that the figures were no more than guesswork anyway.

Be that as it may, nothing came of the project in that form. Instead, the promoters aligned themselves with a proposed Weymouth & Portland Railway. Two such projects were then current, one of which included a harbour tramway. A meeting to consider both was held on 7th October 1861 at the Royal Hotel in Weymouth and it was the one that included the tramway that was adopted, the necessary plans and Bill being approved for the ensuing Parliamentary session. The link between the tramway and the Steam Packet Company remained, the Portland chairman being the same J.A. Devenish while from 1st January 1862 Joseph Maunders, secretary to the Packet Company, was appointed secretary to the Portland company as well, at a salary of £100 a year. Both companies' interests, incidentally, were represented on Weymouth Town Council. Captain William Prowse, R.N., a director of the Packet Company, was currently mayor, Devenish was an alderman and Maunders a councillor.

The meeting carried unanimously a proposal for a deputation 'to wait on the Directors of the Great Western Railway Company with a view to obtain their assistance in carrying out the undertaking' but agreed to hold this in abeyance until the town council had had an opportunity to discuss the project. This they did on 30th December. Opening the discussion, Alderman Devenish stated that 'as all well knew', the want of a tramroad had caused serious injuries to trade in Weymouth. The directors of the Great Western Railway had shown themselves 'highly favourable' to such a scheme; and their engineer, 'the late Mr I.K. Brunel', had felt so strongly on the point that he had included the tramway in his original plan, and would not have brought the line to Weymouth without the tramway being attached.

One member, Councillor Drew, had reservations, saying that while he agreed as to the desirability of a tramroad from the station to the harbour he thought a railway to Portland 'would be a decided injury to the town', leading to the commercial development of Portland Harbour, which would then compete with Weymouth. He regretted that 'both purposes should have been embodied in the same project' and offered 'every support' to a tramway if a railway to Portland were not connected with it. This was an interesting point of view. Each of the two proposed lines, Portland and tramway, was an extension of the Wilts, Somerset & Weymouth but beyond the operational convenience of a single junction with that line they had little in common; 'embodying them in the same project' was no more than expediency. A proposed amendment, that they should be proceeded with separately, received some support but the vote was in favour of the scheme as it stood; and with that the Bill was left to take its course.

CHAPTER TWO

Incorporation

The Weymouth & Portland Railway Company was incorporated on 30th June 1862 (*25 & 26 Vic. cap. 71*), Section 16 of the Act authorising, inter alia, 'a Railway or Tramway to commence by a Junction with (the Portland line) and the Great Western Railway at or near the Junction of (the Portland line) with the said Great Western Railway, and to terminate at or near the Toll House on the Pile Pier in the Parish of Melcombe Regis'.

Before the tramway is considered specifically it may be relevant to give a brief outline of the company generally. The first chairman was J.A. Devenish; the other original directors, all of Weymouth, were Arthur Thomas Pratt Barlow (vice chairman), John William Barrington Browne and William Henry Purcell Weston. The authorised capital was £75,000 — equal to the estimated total cost of the railways authorised — and the Act also conferred borrowing powers for a further £25,000. The actual cost of construction turned out to be £96,120 — perhaps a tenth of which was attributable to the tramway — to which Parliamentary and other expenses added £3,712, bringing the total cost to just within the authorised share and loan capital combined. The contractors were John Aird & Son, of Lambeth. Although promoted locally, to meet local needs, the Weymouth & Portland resembled many other railway schemes of the 1860s in being substantially a contractor's line, Aird & Son subscribing £65,000 of the share capital and the whole of the loan capital, in 5-year debentures at 4½ per cent. In recognition of the firm's stake, John Aird (son) was, in 1867, appointed a director.

By an agreement dated 18th March 1862 and confirmed by the Act the line was to be managed, maintained and worked on completion by a joint committee of the Great Western and the London & South Western, to which companies it was leased in perpetuity at a fixed annual rent of £5,000. To accommodate the traffic of both companies, the Portland line and the tramway were both required to be laid with mixed gauge (*Section 15*).

CHAPTER THREE

Construction and Opening

The course of the tramway from the station yard to the quay was along the water's edge on the Melcombe Regis side of the Backwater (*Map No. 2*), as far as possible utilising Commercial Road, a public thoroughfare. Since no other was feasible, this was the same as had been proposed for each of the four unfulfilled schemes outlined above, though one of those, the Bath & Weymouth, differed from the others, and from the present line, in not running the full length of the quay. Instead, it would have stopped short at the 'George Quay' — i.e., at the George Inn, just above the custom house.

Roughly midway between the yard gates and the pier, the Backwater makes a right-angled bend, known as Ferry's Corner. About 250 yards above the corner, Commercial Road came to an end, the intervening distance being taken up by various commercial and other premises abutting directly onto the water. To bridge this gap, three of the earlier schemes had proposed to build an embankment as

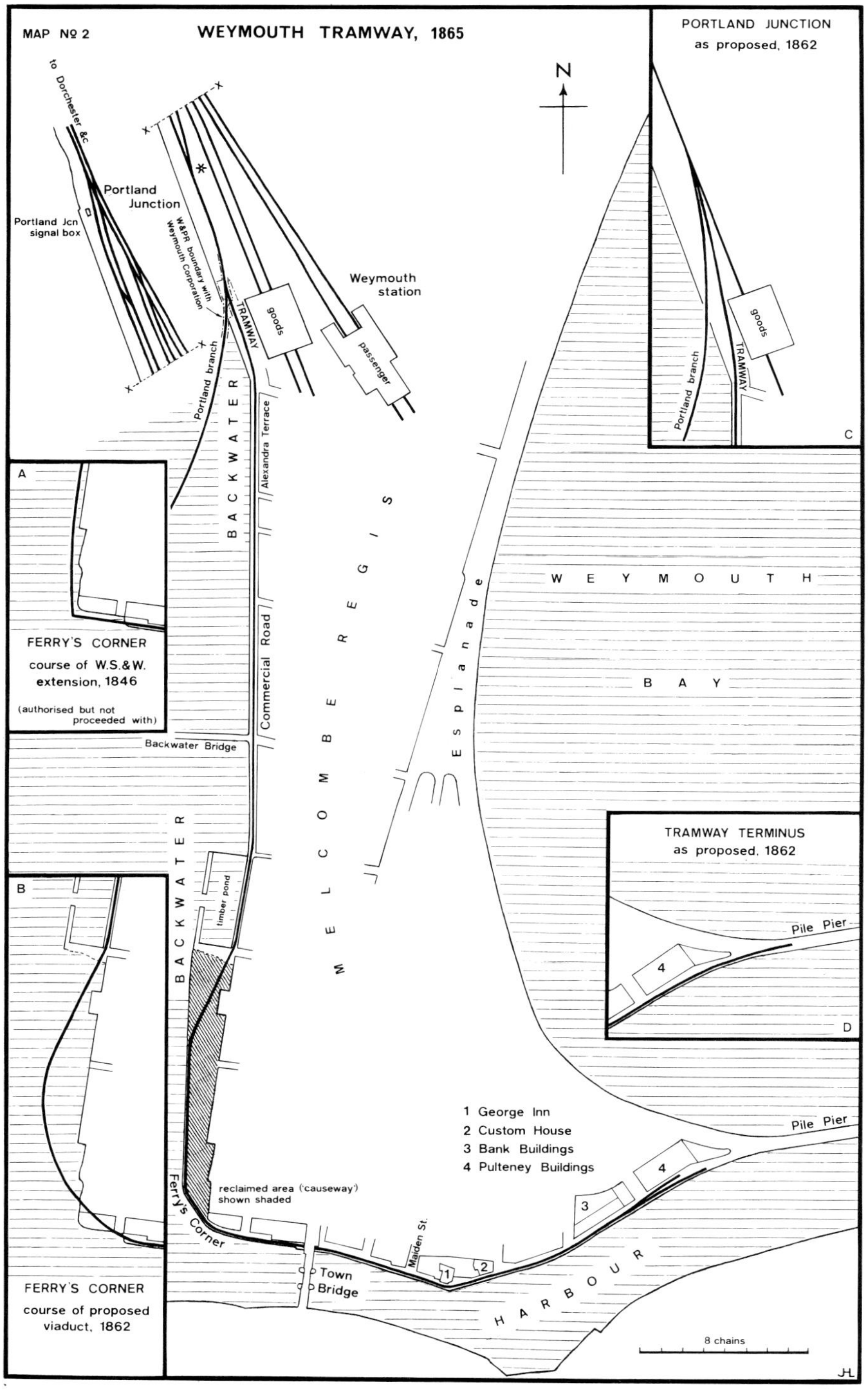

far as the corner and then curve across, to join the existing quay on the other side – two of them on a radius of four chains or thereabouts (involving some demolition of property) and the third, the Exeter line, by a rather sharper curve, skirting the buildings. The exception was the Wilts, Somerset & Weymouth extension, which would have embanked *both* sides of the corner and so kept the line close to the water's edge the whole way. How it was intended to cope with the resulting abrupt change of direction (*Map No. 2, inset A*) is not known; the assumption is a wagon turntable, which would have severely limited the tramway's usefulness.

Improving on both those methods, the Weymouth & Portland proposed to take a wide sweep over the harbour by a wooden pile viaduct, as, indeed, had been envisaged in Devenish's 1861 prospectus; the deposited plan shows one of 8 chains radius and having thirty-seven arches, each of 20ft. span (*Map No. 2, inset B*). In January 1863, however, the company had second thoughts and dropped the idea of a viaduct in favour of an embankment ('causeway'), 'to deepen the waterway and for the benefit of waterside occupiers'. Such substitution was covered by Section 17 of the Act of Incorporation, subject to the consent of owners etc., affected and to the granting of a certificate by the Board of Trade. Weymouth Corporation agreed to the change, 'being satisfied that if the tramway were to be laid upon a solid causeway instead of wooden piles, such alteration would cause an important accretion of land and otherwise materially benefit the property of the Corporation and be an advantage to the public'. Further, the company were granted the right to excavate all necessary materials from the Backwater free of any payment, provided that the work was done under the corporation's supervision; so much of the made land as was actually necessary for the tramway was to be conveyed to the company free of encumbrance whenever they might so request; and, lastly, 'in consequence of the Company executing the works', the corporation undertook to meet all claims for compensation from owners and tenants deprived by the causeway of their direct access to the Backwater. These provisions were incorporated in a memorandum of agreement dated 14th January 1863. The company probably hoped that the 'benefit to waterside occupiers' might be reciprocated, in the way of extra business for the railway, but, whatever the thinking behind it, this reversion to the embankment idea of earlier schemes, with its attendant sharp curve, proved in later years to have been short-sighted. An incidental outcome of the change was to leave more or less intact the workshop premises occupied by James Ferry & Sons (Ferry's Yard) which gave the corner its name.

Just beyond Ferry's Corner was a second obstacle, where the quayside was intersected by the raised approach to the Town Bridge. Passing this involved the building of an archway (the 'tunnel' referred to by Devenish) and raising the level of the road. The existing approach road to the bridge was at an inclination of 1 in 20. Section 23 of the Act of Incorporation authorised this be increased to 1 in 18, to give the necessary clearance underneath, but nearby residents objected. Of various alternatives considered the most interesting was to raise the railway and lower the road, so that they would cross on the level, and replace the existing swing span by a telescopic bridge; but the simplest was merely to limit the extent by which the road was raised. This compromise was accepted. It improved the level of the road, so placating the objectors, but upset the level of the tramway, as proper clearance could be obtained only by making the line dip sharply under the bridge, resulting in a liability to flooding. The rest of the line, for all practical purposes, was level.

The Weymouth & Portland Act established a relationship between the company and Weymouth Corporation that has governed the tramway ever since — a relationship that is, to say the least, unusual. Since it was to run entirely on corporation property (apart from the first few chains, which would be on land owned by the Great Western) the tramway was excluded from the Act's provisions covering the purchase of land. In the circumstances some alternative provision might have been expected, either for the making of agreements with the corporation or for the protection of corporation interests in the event of dispute, but there was none. In their eagerness to see the tramway built, with an eye to harbour revenue, the council in 1862 had entirely neglected such considerations, with the result that the company's authority to lay the tramway on corporation land was unconditional. Avoidance of friction thus depended on community of interest and mutual goodwill.

Work on building the tramway began in October 1862. A year later the engineers, Messrs. Fowler and Ward, were able to report 'the works on the tramway to Weymouth harbour' were 'most satisfactorily progressing'; that 'the bridge under the approach to Weymouth Bridge' had been built, and the traffic turned over it, and 'the laying down of the plates commenced'. Already, however, goodwill was becoming strained, as it was not infrequently to be in years to come. In January 1864 it was reported in council that 'several claims had been sent in asking compensation for deprivation of water access to the Backwater', resulting from the tramway works. There had, too, been numerous complaints about damage suffered by the quay walls (in truth only to be expected, it being generally accepted that the walls were in a very poor state of repair) and about the contractor's failure to clean up properly and make good the road as the works progressed. Misgivings were being increasingly expressed. At a subsequent council meeting, demands were made for the railway to pay for the use of the quays and roads, with a guarantee to cover future repairs, one councillor referring to the council's 'negligence in not watching the progress of the Weymouth & Portland Railway Bill whilst in Parliament'. But the die was cast. The council had indeed not watched the Bill through Parliament. The company's Act did not require them to pay compensation, nor was there any redress for damage.

By May 1864 both Portland line and tramway were finished. Board of Trade inspection of the former, on 19th May, was confidently expected to be followed by the public opening but the need to strengthen two viaducts between Weymouth and Portland and, later, a protracted dispute with the leasing companies over station accommodation at Weymouth, delayed the opening until 16th October 1865. The tramway, of course, was not directly concerned with these arguments, and, as a goods line, was not subject to Board of Trade jurisdiction or inspection, but as an integral part of the Weymouth & Portland it could not be used until they were settled. But for the expediency of 'embodying the two purposes in the same project', it might have been carrying traffic some eighteen months earlier.

The opening, so long awaited, gave the harbour trade a

useful fillip, if only by eliminating the trouble and expense of double handling — first onto road carts and then, at the station, onto rail (or vice versa) — but greater benefit could not be derived as long as the Weymouth line remained encumbered by the broad gauge. It was followed eighteen months later (8th May 1867) by a formal agreement between the company and the corporation, confirming the provisions of the 1863 memorandum and providing for the maintenance by the company of that part of the causeway on which the tramway was laid (a strip about 12ft. wide). To date, claims for compensation totalled £787 16s.4d., and the company's associated costs £115.

As built, the tramway was simply a length of plain line, except at the quay end, where it divided to provide a short siding (*Map No. 2*). This was about 12 chains beyond the custom house, where the steamers berthed and where it was originally proposed the line should end, but 4½ chains short of the pile pier, to which it was authorised (*Map No. 2, inset D*). The distance from the junction as shown on the deposited plan (*Map No. 2, inset C*) was about 79 chains. In fact, the somewhat peculiar arrangement shown, and described in the Act, whereby both the Portland line and the tramway were to diverge from a common point about 170 yards north of Weymouth goods station, was not adopted. Though possibly acceptable for the tramway, whose traffic was expected to be confined to goods, it would hardly have found favour with the Board of Trade for the Portland line, which was to carry passenger traffic as well. Instead, (probably at the instance of the Great Western) a conventional junction with the main line was made at a point 28 chains north of Weymouth Station. Until early in 1899 this was known as Portland Junction; it was then renamed Weymouth Junction. For the first 18 chains or so the branch was used by both Portland and tramway traffic. The two then diverged, the length of the tramway from the point of divergence to the terminus being about 74 chains. Where the two lines diverged the narrow gauge rail 'changed sides', producing a nice example of the complex pointwork so typical of the mixed gauge. The traffic was worked by a local carrier, Charles Jolliffe, using horses, up to four or more being harnessed in line according to the load.

Originally the tramway was laid with special rails but exactly what these were like is something of a mystery. It is on record that for the company's first general meeting, in September 1862, a small model of the 'tramroad to the Quay', and of the 'inverted iron rail' intended to be used, was ordered to be prepared and to be available at the secretary's office for inspection. Whatever its form, the rail appears to have fallen short of expectations. In April 1869, the *Dorset County Chronicle* reported that 'experience has proved that the hollow rails hitherto in use on our harbour tramway do not answer their purpose in consequence of the 'biting' of the wheels of the trucks. Railway metals have therefore been substituted, which will have the effect, it is said, of saving both time and labour'. Other references describe them as 'sunken' rails, suggesting some kind of flanged rail as commonly used on street tramways. The 'railway metals' that were substituted were the normal broad gauge bridge rails, laid on sleepers.

Underneath the Town Bridge, together with the small clearance between broad gauge wagons and the sides of the arch, sleepered track appears to have constituted something of a hazard, resulting in several accidents. In 1870 'the character of the tramway and the mode of its construction' under the arch were strongly criticised by a coroner's jury, as 'very dangerous to persons passing over', especially in the dark. The coroner was also concerned for 'the life of the man employed in driving on this tramway, as a false step while running alongside his horse must inevitably prove fatal'. The corporation referred the matter to the Great Western, who pointed out in reply that the archway was 'never intended as a public thoroughfare' but agreed to place a lamp there, and pay for the gas, and to erect a warning notice at either end.

CHAPTER FOUR

All Traffic Stopped

The shaky state of the quay walls having long been a byword, the Great Western secretary, F.G. Saunders, was probably not entirely surprised when, in June 1873, he received a telegram from the town clerk in Weymouth reading: 'In middle of last night considerable portion of quay wall opposite Maiden St. fell in. All traffic stopped on tram. Many say heavy loads on tram to blame'. A second message, from the engineer's office in Bath, supplied confirmation: 'Two chains of this tramway has gone into the harbour last night. The rails and sleepers have been removed'.

For a month nothing was done, while the corporation tried to prevail upon the Great Western to meet the repair bill; the company, it was said, had promised to send an engineer to inspect the slip, but had failed to do so; and the *County Chronicle* feared for the rest of the wall — that the collapse might prove 'only an instalment' of what was to come. In July Saunders wrote to the town clerk:

> Dear Sir, I am sorry that there has been some unavoidable delay in replying to your letters and telegrams on on the subject of the quay wall at Weymouth, a portion of which has given way — not, I find, from the traffic on the tramway (which I am assured had nothing to do with it), but from the imperfect construction of the masonry of the wall, and its undermining by the sea. The liability to repair the wall does not appear to fall upon this company in any way, and I cannot therefore hold out to the Town Council any hope that my directors will assume the responsibility. If the Town Council should wish to have the opinion of Mr Owen, our engineer, as to the best manner of reconstructing the part fallen down, I have no doubt he will be happy to attend to any communication he may receive from you.
>
> Yours faithfully
>
> Frederick G. Saunders

When the letter was considered in council, the 'anti-tramway' faction was vociferous — there was no doubt the Great Western Railway were running trucks over property never constructed to bear such heavy weights; the council might have to pass a by-law imposing a weight restriction on the line; perhaps, though not legally liable, the company might be prevailed upon to help out . . . but then the cold reality: 'they must look to the support the steamers gave the harbour'. And the opposite view was also put — they could scarcely blame the secretary of the Great Western Railway when it had been stated 'by persons' that the damage had arisen from 'the excavations which the harbour master had made in the harbour' and partly from 'the insecure state of the masonry'. After endless wrangling it was generally admitted that the tramway had been of great benefit to the town and agreed to accept the tender of one Joseph Phillips, for the sum of £1,950. The job took until the following February to complete but it was, said the *County Chronicle*, 'a capital piece of workmanship'. The tramway was reopened in March.

It may be mentioned in passing that in 1902, when the wall showed signs of instability in the vicinity of Alexandra Terrace, and when the consequences of a collapse would have been immeasurably more serious, the Great Western did undertake repairs, in the interests of safety and with the corporation's consent, leaving the question of responsibility to be decided afterwards. The cost was eventually shared, fifty-fifty.

CHAPTER FIVE

Gauge Conversion

Three months after traffic was restored, the long-outmoded broad gauge was dispensed with. Between 18th and 22nd June 1874 the whole of the Wilts, Somerset & Weymouth was narrowed, the broad gauge rails between Dorchester and Weymouth and on the Weymouth & Portland being used for the last time on Thursday the 18th. The actual date of lifting is not known. In respect of the Portland line and the tramway MacDermot (*History of the Great Western Railway*) notes the broad gauge as 'disused' from that date and the broad gauge rails as removed 'soon afterwards' but it would not be surprising if oddments of redundant rail remained in place on the tramway for some time.

The gauge conversion was of particular benefit to Weymouth's Jersey potato traffic — the port's principal cargo — most of which went to the Midlands and north of England and thus, like much of the Great Western's south – north traffic, had been bedevilled by the break of gauge. The following year special potato boats had to be run and the company applied to lay down a siding to accommodate the necessary wagons. The corporation consented provided that the additional rails were only temporary, and that at the end of the season they were lifted and the road restored. The siding was where Cosens's siding was later laid permanently (*Map No. 3*). In subsequent years both this piece of land and the adjoining length (later to be occupied by Greenwood's siding) appear to have been used, and by 1879 there was a slight shift of emphasis — the rails might stay until such time as the corporation decided otherwise. Predictably the sidings provoked complaints and demands for compensation, and in August 1880 Mr Greenwood, the proprietor of Greenwood's Steam Saw Mills (at the end of St. Alban Street) was in trouble with the corporation when he took it upon himself to block the 'inner tramway' in front of his premises — i.e., the siding — with a 3-ton stone.

In a period of about five weeks in the summer of 1876, some 3,500 tons of Jersey new potatoes were landed, a significant increase on previous years. The cargoes were entirely man-handled, there being no quayside crane, and in the light of that season's experience the Packet Company asked the corporation to provide a wooden landing stage, or platform, pointing out in support of the request that a cargo requiring twelve hours for discharge at Weymouth could be dealt with in only five at Littlehampton, where there was such a platform, with a crane.

The corporation were sympathetic but unable to fund the project. The Great Western therefore undertook to meet the cost of construction by advancing £1,000, which would be recovered by withholding wharfage dues on potatoes landed there for as long as might be necessary. An agreement on those lines was signed in April 1877 and the stage, 200ft. long, was completed in time for the coming season; the actual cost was £1,150, the balance being found by the corporation. The Great Western provided a steam crane and the *County Chronicle* was soon reporting record cargoes, involving up to five special boats and 400 tons in one day.

CHAPTER SIX

Introduction of Locomotives

Still, of course, the traffic was all horse-hauled between the quay and the station, and the much heavier tonnages that were now being carried increasingly underlined the limitations of so primitive a practice. It must have been apparent from the outset that unless traffic over the tramway was to be restricted to an unacceptably low level, that situation must arise sooner or later, but the possibility of substituting locomotives had so far been side-stepped, probably for fear of provoking an outcry. Appearing before a Commons committee on the Wilts, Somerset & Weymouth Bill in July 1846, Brunel was asked whether it was intended to work the tramway 'by horse power'. He replied 'yes', and did not elaborate. In the Act, although the 'mixed gauge' clause referred to narrow gauge 'engines and carriages', the form of traction to be employed was not mentioned specifically. The costings put forward in Devenish's draft prospectus tacitly assumed the use of locomotives but when the Weymouth & Portland Bill was in committee the only question asked about the tramway concerned the sharp curvature. That elicited once again the information that the line was 'not intended to be worked by engines', and the matter was not further discussed. As in 1846 the Act was non-committal.

The question was brought to a head in 1878, though not, as might have been expected, by the current demands of the Channel Islands traffic so much as by expectations of further expansion to follow the opening of a new service, to Cherbourg. This had been talked about for some years and plans were now maturing. Among additional facilities required, the one most likely to prove contentious was an engine on the tramway, but here the Great Western were able to invoke aid from an unexpected quarter. The occupants of Pulteney Buildings and Bank Buildings, backing onto the quay, were always complaining about what the *County Chronicle* described as 'the wretched state' in which it was frequently left and 'the noise made by the horses in the summer season from morn to night'. It was suggested that if a 'small engine' were attached to the trucks 'they could be got away . . . and the inconvenience and noise got rid of'.

Further to that suggestion — attributed by some to the mayor but by him to the Great Western — the company wrote to the corporation on 28th February 1878 with reference to what they understood to be 'the desire of the Council and the inhabitants of the borough generally that the tramway between the harbour and the railway station should be worked by a small locomotive'. The letter went on to explain that, before that was possible, additional passing places would be required near the Backwater, and that the company would be glad to know whether the corporation would agree to the tramway being worked by an engine and to the provision of the necessary passing places. Other matters pertaining to the proposed new service were also mentioned but when the letter was discussed in council, at a meeting specially convened, the mayor thought the use of an engine should be considered first.

What was the legal position? The town clerk replied that as to the quay there might be some doubt but that under the company's Act they had no power to put a locomotive on Commercial Road, a public highway. The mayor let that pass, and alluding to the objections that had been raised to trucks being left lying about, horses being there all day, and the nuisance generally, said that if it could all be done away with by the use of 'a small engine consuming its own smoke' he thought it would be most desirable. 'A very great improvement', observed another. Then the voice of dissent — the railway paid not a single penny for running over the quay; the quays saved the Great Western Railway Company a very heavy sum for the transport of their goods from the steamers to the station; the company needed watching. As far as the possibility of damage to the quays was concerned, the mayor had it on 'the most competent authority' that the gradual drawing away of the trucks by an engine would be so smooth and easy that there would be less risk than when horses began to move them. An odd notion, it must be said, but his intentions were good. In reply to a question, the borough surveyor said a locomotive would weigh 'one ton less than a loaded truck'. After prolonged discussion the matter was left over pending a further meeting with the company's officers.

This duly took place on 19th March, when a deputation led by Sir Alexander Wood, the deputy chairman, visited Weymouth. Among those present was William Dean, the locomotive superintendent, and the opportunity was taken to send an engine along so that the town councillors might have a trial trip. The *County Chronicle* provides an engaging account of the proceedings:

> On Tuesday afternoon the Directors of the Great Western Railway Company afforded the Corporation an opportunity of inspecting one of the small locomotives which it is proposed to use on the tramway. To this was attached a composite carriage, consisting of first, second and third compartments, in which sat the Mayor and several members of the Council. The engine, which weighs 12 tons 5cwt., drew the carriage along in the smoothest possible manner and everyone seemed to be of the opinion the quay walls would not be so much injured by it as by the constant jolting of trucks when drawn by horses. The engine proceeded as far as Mr Greenwood's steam saw mills, where a stop had to be made on account of there being a number of empty trucks on the line. It is said the Great Western Railway Company will undertake the sole responsibility in case accident should occur to the public from the use of the engine. Whilst the engine was travelling about four miles an hour one of the members of the Council suddenly got in front of it to ascertain how quickly it could be stopped, and it was brought up almost within its own length.

The importance attached to the Cherbourg service was such that a further meeting was convened only four days later, when the council, impressed by 'the immense advantage this French traffic will confer on the town', agreed to meet all the company's requirements. In particular, it was agreed 'that the Corporation will raise no objection to the use of a traction engine on the quay by the Great Western Railway Company, but with the express understanding that such user takes place at the sole risk and expense of the Great Western Railway Company'. So, whatever the supposed legal niceties, this crucial decision rested in the end on no more than the corporation's consent.

The Cherbourg service started on 1st August 1878. One of the improvements agreed the previous March was an extension of the cargo stage, it being considered impracticable to accommodate both the potato traffic and the new service at the existing stage. Because the new service was regarded as experimental, however, its future was uncertain, and the corporation were reluctant to commit the necessary expenditure. The work was eventually started early in 1880 and completed in May, increasing the length of the stage to 380ft. — practically double the original. The extension was brought into use the following month, on completion of essential alterations to the tramway — extending and combining the two dead-ends to form a run-round loop for engine release (adding about a chain to the tramway's length) and extending the loop westwards to provide extra siding accommodation. These alterations appear to have been spread over a considerable period. Although it is clear from contemporary accounts and correspondence that the 'second line of rails' — i.e., the westward extension of the loop — was in progress during May and June 1880, there is photographic evidence (*Plate 1*) that at least one of the dead ends was lengthened before the stage, presumably in 1878 or 1879. The additional track was required to be laid with guard rails — i.e., check rails — and alongside the original stage kept free of standing trucks because that part of the quay was much used by road vehicles, notably the horse buses carrying steamer passengers to and from the station.

Plate 1: Weymouth Quay, circa 1879, showing the end of the tramway as it was before the extension of 1889 but apparently lengthened slightly from the original terminus of 1865. The cargo stage is as built in 1877; the 1880 extension was along the quay wall towards the camera. The steamer is the *Great Western* (built in 1867), then running between Weymouth and Cherbourg.

Frith, Courtesy Dorset County Museum

Completion of the loop enabled a locomotive to be used, more than two years after the trial. The precise date of first use in ordinary service is open to some doubt. On 5th June 1880 the following paragraph appeared in the *Southern Times*:

> INCREASED FACILITIES FOR TRAFFIC. Owing to the extended amount of traffic the Great Western Railway Company are carrying on at this port it has been found necessary to employ a locomotive to run on the tramway for the purpose of conveying trucks to and from the station, and this was used for the first time on Monday. This is a step in the right direction . . . etc., etc.

In relation to the date of publication 'on Monday' indicates 31st May. Turning to the *County Chronicle*, however, one finds the paragraph in question repeated, word for word, on 10th June, in relation to which 'on Monday' indicates 7th June. The original *Regulations for Working the Weymouth Tramway with Locomotive Engine* (*opposite*) carry the later date, which seems to imply confirmation. It is possible that 31st May was the intended

GREAT WESTERN RAILWAY.

REGULATIONS

FOR

Working the Weymouth Tramway with Locomotive Engine.

THE hours the Engine is to be at work will be regulated by Mr. Collett, the Station Master (who has the General Superintendence of the Tramway), according to the requirements of the traffic, but will be under the immediate orders of Inspector Pollard, who (under Mr. Collett) has charge of the work on the Tramway, and who will be responsible for all regulations with regard to the working of the Engine being strictly carried out.

The Engine must always be accompanied by a Policeman in uniform, who will be responsible for seeing that the road is clear in front of the Engine, and who must warn every one on or about the Tramway of the Engine's approach, and must also see that the Engine does not travel faster than the specified speed. He must either walk in front of the Engine, or ride on the front buffer plank.

In going round sharp curves, and at those places where there are many people or Children on or about the Tramway, the Policeman must always walk a short distance ahead of the Engine, so as to be able to warn people of its approach and to keep the road clear. Where the road is straight, and there are no people about, he may ride upon the Engine.

He must be provided with a Guard's Whistle, and a red flag by day and a Guard's Hand Lamp by night.

The speed of the Engine must not exceed Four miles an hour, and it must travel slower where it is necessary to ensure safety.

The greatest care and vigilance must be exercised, by each person accompanying the Engine and Train, to guard against accident, and ensure the safety of the public; and the Engine Driver must implicitly obey any signal or instruction given by the Policeman.

The Policeman must keep a record of the time of starting and arrival of each trip the Engine makes between the Quay and the Great Western Station, the number of Wagons conveyed each trip, and must make a note of any special circumstance that may occur; these he will enter on a proper Guard's Report at the end of the day, and send in to Mr. Collett.

G. N. TYRRELL,

Superintendent of the Line.

June 7th, 1880.

date and that in the event the engine's introduction was postponed for a week; but equally possible, the date on the regulations notwithstanding, that it was the actual date.

During the next few years further loops were laid in, as shown on Map No. 3. Each of these was subject to a nominal annual wayleave of five shillings (unlike the tramway itself and the cargo stage loop, to which no such charge applied). Two of them are of particular interest. The first is that later known as Templeman's siding, laid down in 1882 and extending from the George Inn eastwards as far as the cargo stage. Between those points the quay was, in places, under 20ft. wide — at its narrowest only about 17ft. Space for the additional track was provided by erecting a wooden staging along the quay wall for a distance of about 450ft., the rails being laid on the staging. In consequence, this siding was subject to a weight restriction, though the terms in which it was stated — no individual truck or engine to exceed 18 tons — took no account of weight distribution or axle loading, normally regarded as critical factors. The other loop of note was at the George Corner. The George Inn, dating from about 1550, projected by some 20ft., causing a serious quayside obstruction and obliging the tramway to adopt a very sharp curve at that point. In 1884 it was bought by the corporation and pulled down, a new 'George' being built further back. This enabled a short loop to be put in, with easier curvature (6 chains radius).

Plate 2: The George Corner circa 1883, shortly before the old building was pulled down.
Author's Collection

The apparent certainty that the Cherbourg service now faced a prosperous future brought forth some elaborate ideas for harbour improvement. One, emanating from W.G. Owen, the Great Western chief engineer, involved a general up-grading of the tramway — even including rebuilding the Town Bridge, to eliminate the dip — and a double track extension to new berths at the pile pier. Plans drawn up by R.P. Brereton, formerly chief assistant to Brunel and now engaged by the corporation as consulting engineer, envisaged docks, either in Weymouth Bay, on the north side of the pier, which would have led to a great increase in traffic over the tramway, or alternatively in the Backwater, which would probably have led to its abandonment. But the service did not prosper; in 1885 it closed down and the grand ideas came to nothing.*

By now there were considerable doubts, too, about the future of the Channel Islands service. The Packet Company's vessels were run down and out of date, capital for replacements was not available, and rumour prophesied closure. In the event, after protracted negotiation and much uncertainty, an agreement was signed on 15th August 1888 whereby the corporation undertook to provide extended facilities (under powers included in the Weymouth & Melcombe Regis Corporation Act, 1887) and the Great Western assumed direct responsibility for the service, with new steamers and connecting trains to the quay.

*for a full account see the author's *The Great Western at Weymouth* (1971)

CHAPTER SEVEN

Passenger Trains

Among the new works for which the corporation were responsible those that affected the tramway were the construction of a landing stage at the pile pier, at rail platform height, with baggage shed and other necessary accommodation 'for the carrying on of a first class passenger service', and widening the quay between the George Corner and the cargo stage by building a new wall in place of the wooden staging erected along the old wall in 1882 (Templeman's siding). Contracts were let in September 1888.

Plate 3: The 'tunnel' through the Town Bridge approach, showing the 1889 widening on the water side of the arch and the wrought-iron arch girders. Note the stone sets and check rails; also (left background) the wagons standing in Farthing's siding. (*See Map No. 3*). The photograph was taken in 1922.

L. A. Wroot

The Great Western were empowered by the agreement to extend and improve the tramway at their own expense (about £2,600). To permit the passage of passenger stock, the arch under the approach to the Town Bridge required to be raised by a foot at the centre. To minimise interference with the road level — a bone of contention in 1862, it may be remembered — the crown of the arch was made thinner by substituting a superstructure of curved wrought-iron girders for the original masonry. This was made in the works at Swindon. At the same time the rail level was lowered by two inches, increasing the height of the arch from 12ft. 4in. to 13ft. 6in. (and also, unfortunately, increasing the tendency to flood). On the side nearer the harbour, the masonry was cut back by 2ft., widening the arch from 12ft. to 14ft.; the track was then slewed by 11¼in. to a new centre line.

The extension to the passenger stage was a single track just over 7 chains long, very much less ambitious than that proposed by Owen in 1884. It was not part of the joint line, covered by the working agreement with the London & South Western, but an easement granted by the corporation to the Great Western alone, subject to an annual wayleave of five shillings. The ground between the rails and for a distance of 2ft. 6in. on either side was required to be pitched with 'the best description of Wood paving blocks laid on Portland Cement concrete . . . laid and maintained . . . to the satisfaction of the Borough Surveyor'. The cost of 'laying and maintaining the whole of the Tramway Sidings and Harbour Branch line . . . to satisfy the requirements of the Board of Trade' was also laid to the Great Western.

Bringing the line to the standard required for passenger trains involved minor realignment at various places between Cosens's siding and the cargo stage, to improve curvature and increase clearances. On Ferry's Corner the worst of the 'angularity' was relieved but the resulting curve, though more regular, still had a radius of only 223ft., even tighter than the 4 chains of some of the early schemes. As a result, bogie stock could negotiate the corner only with

Plate 4: Special loose coupling as used on the tramway from 1889 to 1939. Each link was 16in. long instead of the usual 12in. The photograph was taken in 1959. (*See page 41*).

the ordinary screw couplings disconnected and replaced by special three-link ones, a tedious procedure that was to be endured for the next fifty years. An additional chore when corridor stock appeared, a few years later, was the need to disconnect gangways and lock vestibule doors. (Corridor stock actually appeared on the tramway as early as 1891, when the pioneer vehicles built the previous year were tested with a view to their possible use on the boat trains).

At Portland Junction, the convergence of the up and down branch roads (marked with an asterisk on Map No. 2) was replaced by a scissors crossing, giving separation of the tramway from the Portland line at that point — i.e., about 6 chains north of the original point of divergence (*page 52 plan A*). In connection with this improved layout and the additional signalling and interlocking associated with passenger working, a new 43-lever box was commissioned, a little to the south of the old site. The installation of the scissors crossing and the opening of the pier extension combined to increase the length of the tramway to 1 mile 8 chains (the odd chain having already been added to the original 74 chains by the cargo stage loop). As is well known, the 'baulk road' remained in use long after the disappearance of the broad gauge, and it is of passing interest that the Portland scissors crossing was among the very last examples. It was not relaid with standard rail and sleepers until 1910.

Plate 5: Weymouth Junction Box, opened in 1889. This photograph was taken in September 1956, shortly before the box was closed. The new box can be seen in the background. After this was opened, in April 1957, the word 'junction', in reference to the main line end of the tramway, was dropped.

In February 1889, the contractors for the new quay wall (Sanders, of Westminster) complained that they were being hampered by traffic on the tramway. For some weeks all movement of goods between the station and the quay therefore reverted to road cartage. The stopping of traffic over the tramway no doubt had the additional advantage of facilitating reconstruction of the Town Bridge arch. For the seasonal potato traffic, however, cartage was regarded as impracticable, so from May until the beginning of July work on the wall was stopped instead, enabling the tramway to be reopened. On 20th June it was tested for passenger traffic. 'For this purpose', the *County Chronicle* records, 'one of the largest coaches — an eight-wheeler — was attached to the tramway engine and conveyed from the station to the staging. The coach cleared everything, but a few alterations will have to be made in the removal of telegraph poles etc.'

By the terms of the agreement the new facilities were required to be ready, and the new steamers available, by 1st July 1889, but for various reasons neither the corporation nor the Great Western succeeded in keeping to that date. Delay in completing the new quay wall was to be expected because of the suspension of work during the potato season, but progress on other contracts, notably dredging, was also disappointingly slow. On the tramway, too, some work was still outstanding on the appointed date, and the first of the new steamers did not reach Weymouth until 21st July. During July, the working agreement with the Packet Company having expired on 30th June, an interim service was run by two old Great Western paddle steamers (*Gael* and *Great Western*), with nothing better than the existing bus connection between the station and the quay.

On 29th July the town clerk met Henry Lambert, the Great Western general manager, and assured him that even though some work remained to be done the new service could now start, whereupon Lambert, much relieved, said that he would arrange inspection of the tramway for Friday 2nd August and commencement of the new service for the 3rd. The inspector for the Board of Trade was Major General Hutchinson (*see page 30*).

The first outward sailing by one of the new steamers (*Lynx*) took place on Sunday 4th August 1889. Through trains to the quay began at the same time (not, as has often been stated, on 1st July), the first passenger train to use the tramway being the 9.15p.m. from Paddington on Saturday, 3rd August, connecting with the 2.10a.m. departure on the 4th, and the first up train the 3.45p.m. from the quay on Monday the 5th. Board of Train sanction — the necessary 'confirmation in writing' — was conveyed to the company formally on 8th August, four days after the trains started running. They first appeared in the public time table with the next issue, the following October.

Regular passenger traffic, albeit as yet on a limited scale, served to confirm the tramway's unique character, and set a new pattern for its working. Apart from some small variations in siding accommodation, no further development 'on the ground' occurred for more than forty years. It is therefore convenient at this juncture to digress, and give some account of day-to-day operating.

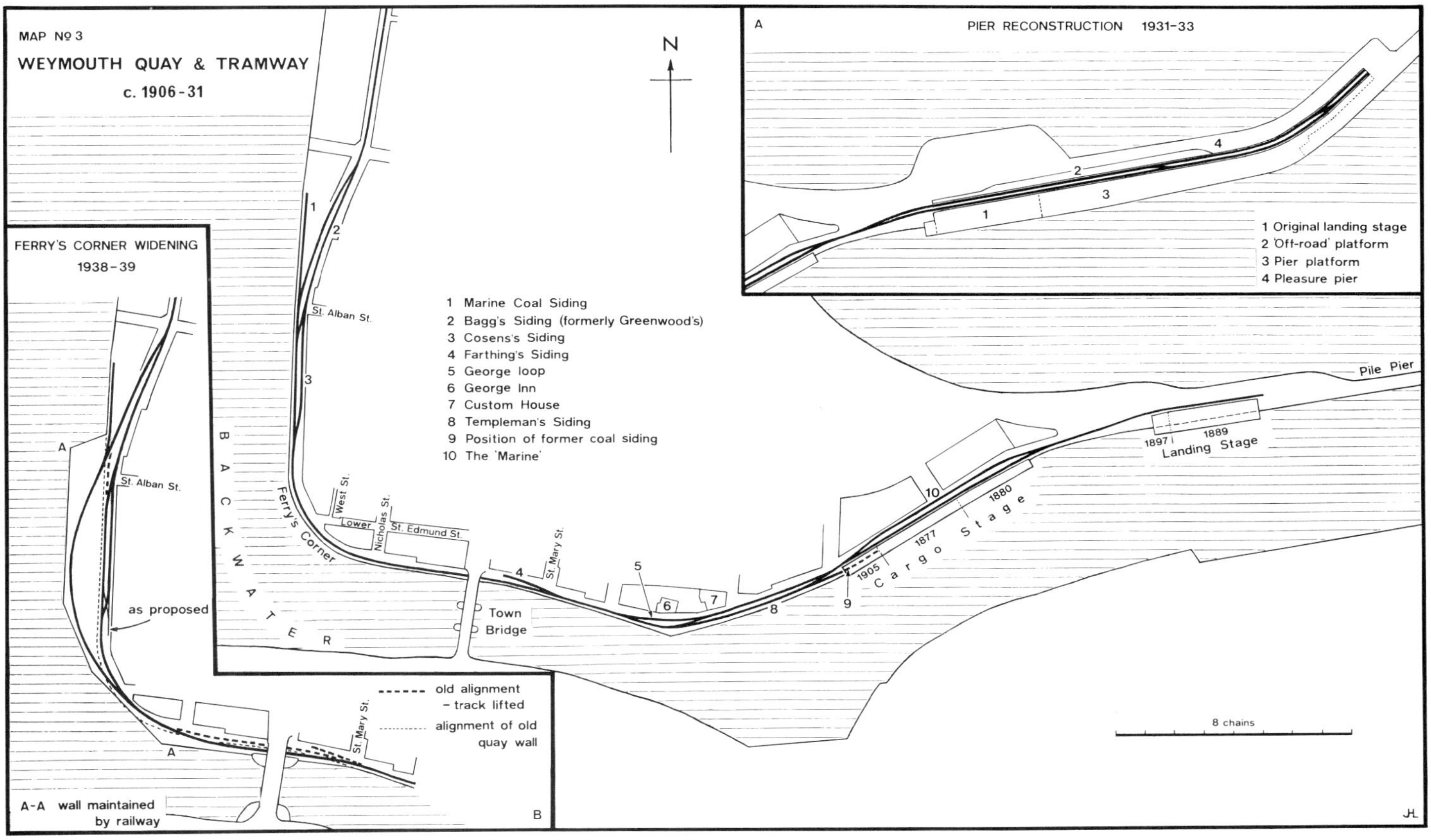

THE LANDING STAGE

Plate 6: An 1889 view: the boat train consists of three non-corridor 'eights' headed by one of the Bristol & Exeter tanks (*see page 57*), and the steamer is one of the three put into service that year (*Lynx*, *Antelope* or *Gazelle*).

Author's Collection

Plates 7 & 8: Circa 1909: (i) The train is again headed by one of the Bristol & Exeter tanks. Note the 'hook' step and post hand-hold (*see page 81*). (ii) In this view the engine is No. 1386, ex-Whitland & Cardigan Railway. In each case the train consists of six carriages, two of which project off the end of the platform (*see page 31*).

(i) *Author's Collection*
(ii) *Seward, Weymouth*

Plate 9: September 1921: the steamer, *Reindeer,* has just come alongside. This view shows very clearly the wood-block paving between the rails and on either side. Note also the GW&LSW Joint parcels van, the Post Office van and the waiting taxis.

British Rail

Plate 10: A model-maker's view, showing interesting details of rolling stock and of the 1889 baggage shed.

Author's Collection

Plate 11: The Channel Islands boat train on arrival at the landing stage, circa 1906, with all but the first four carriages trailing back along the quay as far as the cargo stage. The carriage roof board reads THROUGH CARRIAGE PADDINGTON AND WEYMOUTH. The gentleman in the panama hat (right foreground) is Capt. H.W. Hemmings, the company's Assistant Marine Superintendent. Note the wide gaps between the carriages, owing to the use of the special tramway couplings, and passengers alighting by wooden steps (though the gentleman in the fourth compartment prefers to jump down).

Author's Collection

Plates 13 & 14: Commercial Road: (i) Looking North, towards the goods yard. Note the unmade surface and track without check rails. Left background — the Backwater Viaduct (Portland branch). (ii) At the junction with King Street. The vans standing in the loop (*see Plan A, page 52*) were probably awaiting movement to the quay. Left — the Backwater Viaduct; right — the goods shed. Both photographs were taken about 1906. Where it flanked the railway and Commercial Road the Backwater has been progressively reclaimed (*compare Maps Nos. 1 and 2*).

Author's Collection

Plate 12 (Left): This photograph, showing an interesting array of LNWR rolling stock, is thought to have been taken on 16th June 1904, when 15,000 birds were sent to Weymouth in two trains, totalling 44 vehicles, by the East Lancs. Federation of the Homing Pigeon Society. Their embarkation on board the steamer *Reindeer* was watched with considerable interest, said the *County Chronicle*. Pigeon traffic remained a feature of the summer working until about 1964.

Author's Collection

Plate 15: The year is 1932; the nightmare of modern traffic is still in the future and Commercial Road enjoys an almost rural tranquility. This view, photographed on 29th June of that year, shows the tramway between Webb Major's siding and Westham crossing.

British Rail

Plate 16: The George Corner circa 1922 — the tramway full of wagons and the harbour full of ships. The railway steamers present are the *Great Western* (stern-on, right centre) *Ibex* and, in the distance, at the landing stage, either the *Roebuck* or the *Reindeer*.

Seward, Weymouth

CHAPTER EIGHT

Working the Tramway

Embracing the Portland line and the tramway in a single Parliamentary Act was no more than expediency, as has been remarked, and their dissimilarity was reflected in the different arrangements made by the leasing companies for their working. Portland passenger traffic, though worked for various periods by the Great Western, was predominantly a South Western preserve, while each company worked its own goods traffic; and finally, after the Grouping, the Southern Railway took over the working entirely. As far as operating was concerned the Great Western's interest may therefore be said to have been a minority one.

On the tramway the opposite was the case, to the South Western's virtual exclusion. It is possible that in the line's earliest days a South Western horse ventured down Commercial Road on occasion but that possibility apart the tramway was always worked by the Great Western. In all but name it *was* Great Western, and even before the 1888 agreement was generally so regarded. When the quay wall fell down, for instance, the matter was referred to Paddington, not Waterloo; and the temporary sidings — indeed some of the permanent loops — were agreed by the corporation with the Great Western alone, and at Great Western expense.

The South Western's detachment was logical. The bulk of the traffic on the tramway was associated with the cross-channel steamers, and the South Western's cross-channel business was well established at Southampton, in competition with Weymouth. South Western traffic using the tramway was therefore limited to wagons for one or other of the waterside premises served 'in passing', and those could be handled equally well by the Great Western. The issue of joint working did not arise. A wry consequence was that when the cargo stage loop was being laid down, and a resident of Pulteney Buildings, concerned at the 'further encroachment', complained to both companies, it transpired that the South Western knew nothing about it. Unabashed, the Great Western decided to ask the South Western to pay half the cost. Although the sum was small — half of £149.18s. — the response was possibly cool. If only for the sake of appearance, later agreements usually included the South Western, and in at least one further case (Greenwood's siding), that company was asked to meet half the cost.

A picture of early working practice, in horse-drawn days, comes down to us through an incident that occurred one day in 1877. An old man who had gone to the station yard to buy three-halfpenny worth of coal stopped on the track, inside the yard gates, to pick up some 'slag' (coal waste). Sadly, he failed to notice a rake of wagons being propelled towards Commercial Road. At the inquest, the engine driver:

> I was shunting some trucks with my engine from the goods yard onto the tramway . . . the whistle being blown all the time to warn any people who might be going over the level crossing, and which is always done. We then stopped dead with the trucks, and the porter uncoupled the Portland train from the tramroad trucks. I then gave the signal to go ahead and stopped at Mr. Jolliffe's coal wharf, where a truck was left; went ahead on the Portland loop, then unhooked the engine, went round the train, and proceeded to Portland . . . there were twenty-six trucks being shunted, but these did not go beyond the gate. The porter who had to uncouple the trucks was riding on one of them — on the sixth or seventh from the engine. It was impossible either for me or the porter to see anyone in front of the trucks. I have been driving for two years and do all the shunting. No trucks have been shunted flying down the tram for the last two years, as I thought it a dangerous practice. No one has ever warned me but I did not like the look of the thing. This used to be done, but then the speed was not very sharp — not over four miles an hour — he must have been knocked down by the tail end of the train. It is impossible to make a flying shunt on the tramway although it is possible for me to drive the trucks sharply and then let them go by themselves but this had not been done for the last two years. I have never seen the trucks run down the tram unattended. On the day in question the fireman, porter, and guard were riding on them.

The fireman confirmed that trucks were always coupled to the engine and never detached until brought to a dead stop; but a resident of Alexandra Terrace (*Map No. 2*) did not agree:

> The trucks go very fast past my house when they are shunted, and it is a very dangerous practice. I have seen trucks pass my house with no one in charge of them; I have known them run down as far as the timber yard, not attached to any engine or any one attending them . . . the engine being at the gate. I saw the engine push the trucks and then go back. I cannot say how many trucks passed my house, but I should think twelve or fourteen.

The foreman porter:

> I was in the brake van next to the engine. The train was composed of twenty-one trucks for the tramway, three for Portland, Jolliffe's truck of coal, brake van, and engine. That is not an unusual number — sometimes there are more, sometimes less . . . the train was stopped dead before the wagons were detached . . . have never known the engine give the trucks a violent push . . . the engine never passed the gate.

Mr J.P. Collett, the Great Western station master (until 1912 there were two Weymouth station masters, each company appointing its own), admitted that two years previously his attention had been drawn to the practice of trucks being driven along the tramway detached from the engine:

> Seeing the great danger arising from this . . . I gave instructions that violent shunting should be stopped . . .

it is contrary to practice to allow the engine to come through the gates, on account of the weakness of the quay which supports the tram . . .

Other residents of Alexandra Terrace then came forward to say that they had complained 'fifty times' about trucks running loose down the tram, but that things had not improved. How was a man riding on the twenty-first truck from the end to see what was on the tramway? Some years previously men had been placed at intervals, especially along the terraces of houses, to direct the line, but within the last two or three years that had not been done, neither had there been any man riding on the first truck . . . or in a position to see whether the line was clear or not . . . the trucks went by at a terrific rate.

The jury returned a verdict of accidental death, but added a rider as to the need for caution in shunting. Asked by the coroner whether it would be possible to place a man with a red flag on the line and another in the foremost truck, Mr Collett replied that certainly it could be done if thought desirable.

The shunting procedure described is of much interest. Despite the denials we may be fairly sure that it often did involve loose shunting down the tramway — the temptation to 'knock 'em up', to shorten horse haulage, must have been strong; and the evidence smacks very much of 'doth protest too much'. On the other hand, the complainants were living in an age happily remote from modern traffic, and must have seen the shunting as a worse hazard than it might appear to modern eyes. Also of interest is the make-up of the train, nearly all the wagons being for the tramway, only three for Portland.

All the evidence about loose shunting was, of course, irrelevant to the accident — a point made by the coroner. The man had been inside the yard gates and was therefore a trespasser; but a hundred years and more later we are indebted to the inquest, and to the Victorian newspapers which recorded such matters so meticulously, for a commentary that we should otherwise not have had. Fate has ensured the old man a posthumous niche in railway history: his name was Thomas Smith.

The change to locomotive haulage on the tramway was accompanied by the issue of specific instructions, as already mentioned (*page 17*). The policeman with his red flag or handlamp perhaps owed something to the incident just recounted; such regulations are often born of hard experience. A re-issue dated July 1880 suggested a certain touchiness on the part of the South Western at seeing Great Western control of the tramway endorsed in this way. The revised version was headed JOINT WEYMOUTH TRAMWAY instead of GREAT WESTERN RAILWAY and concluded with the unoffending BY ORDER, without specifying whose. The main wording remained unchanged but the working of the engine was now to be 'regulated according to the requirements of the Great Western and South Western companies . . . without undue preference'. The need to study the convenience of traders loading and unloading trucks at 'Stores on the Tramway' was also mentioned.

How far 'policeman' should be interpreted literally is possibly open to question. If the duty described ever was undertaken regularly by a uniformed constable, it appears not to have been for very long, as by 1882 the tramway staff was stated to consist of driver, fireman, shunting foreman and flagman, under the direction of the quay inspector. It appears, moreover, that in practice trains were not always preceded even by the flagman, and that the speed limit was often exceeded, as, for example, when the engine 'came round the George Corner and before it could be stopped struck the shore end of the plank being used to unload a coal ship'. The distance from the corner to where the ship was reported to be lying is 50 yards or more. Perhaps the rails were wet!

At first the engine appears to have been used solely — or at any rate mainly — to haul wagons to and from the station, it being noted at the time that a horse was to be kept on the quay 'for the purpose of shifting the trucks backwards and forwards to keep the line as clear as possible'; but by 1886 — probably earlier — two engines were allocated to Weymouth for the tramway and one may assume that as the traffic increased so did dependence on the tram engines. Horses, supplied by the Great Western's outside cartage contractors, were not entirely dispensed with until early in the present century, however; in fact, shunting with horses was still referred to in the tramway working regulations until as late as 1931.

The dangerous practice of propelling wagons ahead of the engine without a proper look-out persisted for some time, and in 1887 was the cause of another death, that of a small boy. The inquest jury were told that 'no one was walking in front', and the coroner commented, in the presence of both station masters, that trains on the tram often exceeded four miles an hour and that he did not think the flagman had carried out his instructions. The foreman of the jury said they wished to 'condemn the practice of putting trucks in front of the engine', and were 'of opinion the flagman should walk the whole distance in front of the train'. The coroner referred the matter to the town council, saying 'I concur in the opinion expressed', but when the council in turn referred it to the Board of Trade, asking for action to be taken, the Board pointed out in reply that as the tramway appeared to be used for goods and not passenger traffic it did not come within the description of a railway or tramway requiring inspection. The recommendation appears, nevertheless, to have borne fruit, as propelling was afterwards prohibited as a normal method of working.

The most significant changes were those brought about by the introduction of passenger trains. The steamers were the responsibility of the Marine Department, in the person of an assistant marine superintendent (the company's marine superintendent being based at New Milford, for the Irish traffic), but the landing stage, like the tramway, came under the authority of the station master, who was required to meet the incoming steamer personally 'to superintend the discharge of passengers, parcels and luggage' and 'the dispatch of the train from the pier and from the junction, travelling with it when necessary between those points'. At first only the passenger trains used it. A limited relaxation, to enable potatoes carried by the mail steamers to be landed there, was granted in 1892 but until then the corporation would not allow goods wagons to go beyond the cargo stage. Alongside the cargo stage, the original line became a loop and the erstwhile loop the through road to the pier. In operating terms these were known respectively as the 'Stage' and the 'Marine', though when those names were first used is not known.

The pier platform was just long enough to accommodate four carriages, which formed part of an ordinary Weymouth working, the town and quay portions being divided or combined at Portland Junction. After the departure of the

2.10a.m. outward boat, the carriages remained at the platform to await the inward boat at 3.15p.m. the following day. More intimate details of the working in the early years of the passenger service are included in a letter of 1895 from one John Birks, thought to have been a locomotive inspector, to Thomas Simpson, the outdoor assistant in the Locomotive and Carriage Department at Swindon:

December 7th, 1895

Dear Sir,

Shunting Engine, Weymouth Quay

The following is a general statement of the every day working of the engine booked out at 2.0p.m. and taken charge of by a Pilotman, goes down at once and clear the Tramway and bring back any traffic which can be got at.

At 3.0p.m. D. Elkins take charge and takes down any Fruit Vans & Customs goods that may be on hand to the Cargo staging. Engine then proceeds to the Pier Station & is attached to the Boat train which it takes to Portland Jc., return light to the Quay & bring up the Fruit Vans for 5.20 passr. train, afterwards take down General Goods and return with Perishable Goods for 7.20 express London Goods down to the Quay again with any L&SW Co's traffic or any that may be on hand, does shunting at the stage & bring away any surplus empties to the Station. Meets 12.45p.m. Chippenham Goods & takes down & berths its traffic return again to station & takes traffic off 11.05a.m. Bristol Goods & the steam coal for the company's boats. A sampling of the empty wagons for next day's use by the traders is made and what are not required are taken to the station. The engine then waits the arrival of the Down Boat train due 1.45a.m., proceed to the Pier afterwards run round the train & propells it back into position for the afternoon. It then proceeds to berth the wagons selected for the days use and returns to shed about 3a.m.

I have watched the working for last night and although not exactly to the programme on account of the Boat Train having a late start the men were fully occupied at their work & I fail to see that any improvement or save can be effected even with the road put in good condition, unless accompanied by a large increase in siding accommodation.

I may mention that one engine does the work for both companies & that a great deal of time is occupied in shunting the Merchants with the class of stock they require from both companies.

Yours truly
sgd. Jno. Birks

Thos. Simpson Esq.

What occasioned the letter is not known but it may be inferred that questions had been asked about what we should now call productivity. Although the air of breathless activity conveyed owes something to the letter's sparse punctuation, one certainly gets the impression that No. 1376 (or was it 1377? – *see page 57*) was earning its keep. 'Shunting the merchants' involved not only the private commercial premises served by the loops but port traffic other than the Great Western's own. These extra traffics, not covered by through rates, were liable to a tramway toll (*see Appendix IV*). David Elkins was the regular tramway driver at the time.

Plate 17: An unusual example of 'private siding' traffic. In April 1903 Sir Thomas Lipton's yacht *Shamrock III* was dismasted while practising in Weymouth Bay for the 'America's Cup' races. The broken mast, 170ft. long, was brought ashore on barges by Cosens & Co. and, after the removal of all reusable fittings, loaded away for scrap. It is seen here, loaded on a line of twin timber trucks. standing on the tramway outside Cosens's premises (Cosens's siding to the right). The gentleman in the bowler (left) is Mr F.G. Davies, GWR station master; next to him (in Norfolk jacket) is Mr M.C. Frowde, of Cosens & Co.; and in the foreground the portly figure of Inspector John Gill (*see page 123*).
Author's Collection

The engine's roster was governed by the steamer times — i.e., off shed in time for the inward boat and the up boat train and back on shed on completion of 'tidying up' following the sailing of the outward boat. The potato traffic in season required an engine to be booked out to cover the earlier part of the day as well, which probably involved two separate rosters (that was certainly the case in later years). One can only regret that no comparable account is available for, say, a day in June.

The reference to the engine going down 'to clear the tramway', in charge of a pilotman, relates to wagons left in the loops for commercial users. These were apt to be moved foul of the points so before a passenger train was permitted to run over the tramway the 'duly appointed Tramway Shunter in charge' was required to take a light engine over the line to ensure that it was clear.

This was one of several requirements to ensure passenger safety. An inevitable consequence of the introduction of passenger traffic was that it brought the tramway within the jurisdiction of the Board of Trade; the inspection of 1889 has already been mentioned. Unusually — a reflection of the highly unusual circumstances — the Board directed Major General Hutchinson to visit the tramway while passenger trains were still only a proposal. His report, dated 23rd February 1889, makes interesting reading. After observing that the streets along which the tramway ran were unimportant, with little vehicular traffic; that passenger trains would 'as a rule' run only twice a day; and that it was proposed that 'a man on foot with a red flag should in all cases precede the engine, whereby the speed must necessarily be restricted to about 4 miles an hour' (i.e., as already provided for in the instructions) he expressed no objection to the proposal 'upon the distinct understanding as to speed' and provided that certain other requirements were met. Some of these were already embodied in the 1888 agreement; the more significant additions were:

1. That the Portland loop be worked as a proper double line, with appropriate signalling (given effect by the construction of the scissors crossing);
2. That safety points worked by weighted levers be provided for all sidings;
3. That sharp curves be kept a full inch slack of gauge;
4. That the engine carry a bell which should ring as the train advanced.

The last was to remain a characteristic of tramway working for more than ninety years, and is of particular interest. The speed limit, dating from the start of locomotive haulage, was imposed originally in the interests of other road users but in respect of a passenger train it became equally relevant to the safety of the train. In August, when the inspector made his second visit, representatives of Weymouth Corporation who were present expressed themselves satisfied with the precautions prescribed.

The 1889 Regulation of Railways Act, Section 1 of which empowered the Board to order the adoption of block working, with interlocking of points and signals, on any railway open for the public conveyance of passengers, came into force on 30th August 1889, just after passenger traffic started, but no order was issued in respect of the tramway. In 1924, when the Ministry of Transport decided to issue new orders 'across the board' — i.e., superseding all those issued before the Grouping — the Great Western applied for the existing exception in respect of the tramway, as established in 1889, to continue. Exemption from the provisions of the Act was authorised in accordance with the Ministry of Transport (Great Western and Southern Railway Companies Safety Regulations) Order, 1925, confirming piloting and the weighting (in practice spring-loading) of all points serving sidings, so that their normal position was open for the tramway. Inherent in piloting were the 4m.p.h. speed limit and the rule that a passenger train 'must in every case be drawn in both directions'. Between the station and a point about 120 yards above the Town Bridge, 'one engine in steam' was — and remains — the rule, more than one engine or train being permitted between there and the pier subject to certain safeguards. The point in question was for many years marked by a CAUTION board, referred to incorrectly in the tramway instructions as being opposite Nicholas Street; it was actually at the end of Lower St. Edmund Street (*see Map No. 3*). It disappeared during or shortly after the 1939 war.

Communication between the quay and the station was maintained during the early days of passenger working by the tramway inspector, with recourse to the telegraph when necessary *(p. 123)*. In due course this was superseded by a telephone link between the junction and the quay, resulting

Plate 18: The caution board, opposite the end of Lower St. Edmund Street.

British Rail

in a form of control that has been described as a combination of time-interval working and telephone block. When this was first established is not known but it was probably not later than about 1900.

Traffic grew steadily. A general authority for the pier to be used for cargo when the stage was fully occupied was given in 1897 and, on the passenger side, the regular night service was augmented in summer by a sailing in the middle of the day. At first this was only on Saturdays but from 1897 it became daily. Holiday-makers liked being able to travel both ways in daylight and in summer (though not in winter) Weymouth became the more popular route. One result of increased traffic was that in May 1899 the working of the quay was transferred to the Marine Department. At about the same time an inspector (under the station master) was given specific responsibility for the tramway — an indication of its growing importance. In consequence of these changes, the station master was no longer required to meet the boat every day and travel up the tramway with the boat train.

The landing stage platform was by now inadequate for the summer traffic, '88 wheels', the maximum load then permitted on the tramway, trailing back along the quay all the way to the cargo stage. Only those passengers in the first four carriages could alight or board normally. The rest were accommodated at rail level by the use of portable steps. This inconvenience could be alleviated by berthing the boat train alongside the cargo stage, and on Saturdays it was not uncommon for that to be done. The normal procedure was for the steamers to load cargo there and then move down to embark passengers at the pier, but sailing direct permitted cross-platform transfer for all as well as saving time. The steps nevertheless remained very much part of the tramway scene. Not only was the cargo stage frequently unavailable, but incoming passengers were obliged to use the pier anyway, as the stage had no customs facilities. Passengers boarding at the stage other than from the boat train also used them, to get onto the stage.

As operation of the tramway became more complex so, inevitably, did the relevant regulations and instructions. The last issue under the authority of the leasing companies jointly appears to have been in 1887. The July 1889 revision, covering the introduction of passenger trains, bore the name of N.J. Burlinson, the Great Western superintendent of the line, and thereafter the regulations became part of the sectional appendix to the Great Western service timetables. By 1920, if not earlier, the original single sheet of 1880 had expanded to occupy fully six pages of the appendix. The relevant pages from the May 1931 appendix are reproduced here in full as Appendix 1 (*page 118*).

Certain less familiar aspects of tramway working as it used to be are revealed in an old Weymouth station register that has survived. Among much other fascinating detail of the life of the station, the register provides a comprehensive record of staff and staff duties in the Nineties and later. Items pertaining to the tramway are reproduced as Appendix II *(page 123)*.

THE CARGO STAGE

Plate 19: Passengers going aboard from the boat train on a summer Saturday, circa 1910. The steamer double-berthed with the *Reindeer* (1897) is the *Ibex* (1891).

Author's Collection

Plates 20 & 21: Two further views of about the same date, but showing cargo working: (i) Jersey potatoes. (ii) Export beer; the engine is *Hook Norton (see page 60)* and the steamer the *Roebuck* (1897).

Author's Collection

Plate 22: A September 1921 view: Guernsey tomatoes being unloaded from the cargo steamer *Pembroke*, with wagons double-banked through the 'Stage' and the 'Marine'. At this time the old method of packing the tomatoes, in returnable baskets, was giving way to the cheaper, non-returnable, wooden 'chip', and this cargo includes both.

British Rail

Plate 23: A 1929 view: wagons again double-banked through both roads as far as the eye can see. This time the cargo is French broccoli, brought from various small Breton ports by independent cargo steamers, one of which, the Walford Lines vessel *Jolly Hugh*, is berthed alongside.

Author's Collection

Plate 24: Broccoli boats often discharged at the passenger landing stage. In this 1930 view the 25-kilo crates are stacked high in the roadway on either side of the tramway. The gentleman in the bowler is Mr Percy Boyle, GWR Traffic & Marine Agent at Weymouth from 1916 to 1935, accompanying Mme. Gauttier, representing the French growers.
Author's Collection

Plate 25: A similar view, of about the same date, but this time the broccoli wagons have the tramway to themselves. The steamer is one of the regular broccoli boats, the Care Lines vessel *Porthcarrack*.
Courtesy B. Crump

CHAPTER NINE

Later Developments

The increase in traffic that began in 1889 continued more or less unabated until, by the early twenties, it had reached saturation point. During that time there had been only two small additions to facilities, a 40ft. extension of the pier landing stage in 1897, to accommodate larger steamers, and a further 100ft. on the cargo stage in 1904/5. Because only four carriages could stand at the landing stage a full-length train interfered with cargo working; lack of space resulted in much additional shunting; and some traffic was having to be refused altogether. More specifically, on the tramway, operation was still hampered by such archaic practices as loose couplings and portable steps. The feasibility of large-scale works now began to receive active consideration.

Before these are described, however, a further word

Plate 26: The boat train at the landing stage in August 1929. The train is modern, as is the steamer (*St. Julien*, 1925) but in essentials the scene has changed little during the previous twenty five years. The train includes two of the triplet articulated sets of 1925 but still trails along the quay, needing portable steps for access. Note the break between the triplet sets, to permit freedom of movement across the track; also the carriage roof boards.

British Rail

needs to be said about the cargo stage extension. This took in a spur at the end of Templeman's siding which had been used since 1889 as the marine coal siding, coal being transferred there to the barges that took it down to the ships' berths. The extension was subject to agreement dated 13th April 1899 and at the same time the company entered into agreement with Mr John Bagg, the proprietor of a timber yard alongside the Backwater, to lease a strip of land for a new coal siding at a rent of £20 a year* — a rather different proposition from the usual five-shilling corporation wayleave (*Map No. 3*). (As the land was corporation owned, both the lease and the rent were subject to corporation consent). Before the site could be used the harbour alongside had to be dredged and the wall strengthened. Incredibly, nearly four years elapsed before that work was completed and the new siding brought into use, work on the stage being correspondingly delayed.

Loading the coal barges at the new siding took some of the pressure off the lower end of the tramway. A further advantage was that a source of dust and dirt was removed from a sensitive area, near dwelling houses. The coal siding was often referred to locally as Stockton's siding, after the man who was for many years coal foreman, Fred Stockton. After 1932 it was no longer required for coaling but remained in use as an ordinary traffic siding until about 1947.

A first draft plan for the complete reconstruction of the pier was prepared in January 1925, but six years and several revisions passed before agreement between the corporation and the Great Western was formally sealed (31st December 1930). It provided for a new pier, roughly on the line of the old one but wide enough for a double-track extension of the tramway, extending over the greater part of its length, and two platforms (*Map No. 3, inset A*).

*about £800 at 1985 prices.

Plate 27: The approach to the pier during reconstruction, photographed on 13th April 1932, showing the existing 'pier road' (right) and points for the new 'off road' (left).

British Rail

As in 1888 responsibility was split, the corporation being responsible for the structure and buildings (with the support of a twenty-year Great Western guarantee on the loan charges) while the Great Western undertook to provide and maintain the permanent way, cranes and crane tracks. The contract was placed with the Birmingham firm of Bolton & Lakin and work started in February 1931 under the general superintendence of a resident Great Western engineer. The official opening was performed by the Prince of Wales on 13th July 1933.

The effect of the reconstruction was to increase the length of the tramway by about 12 chains. Each track could hold about fifty wagons or a full length passenger train. Two crossovers were provided, one at the end, for engine release, and the other intermediately. Electric capstans (the modern equivalent of 'a horse to shift the trucks backwards and forwards'?)(*page 28*) were installed but never used, and shortly afterwards were removed. The existing landing stage and baggage shed were incorporated into the new structure.

After years with no room to 'swing the cat', the quay staff must have found all the extra space almost an embarrassment. Certainly it was of immediate benefit. The Birmingham (summer Saturdays) boat train could now be worked through to the quay as well as the Paddington trains, instead of having to use the town station, and the following year an additional one was introduced, from Bristol. Much of the cargo working was also transferred to the new berths, modern electric cranes being a marked advance on the steam-driven antiques that served the cargo stage.

Portable steps were now a thing of the past but two other operating hindrances, loose couplings and the need to disconnect gangways, remained (though alleviated to some extent by the use of articulated stock, introduced in 1925). Disconnected gangways were also a potential source of danger. Passing through the train as the empty stock was being worked back to the junction one night, a shunter slipped between two carriages and was killed. Widening the curve at Ferry's Corner, to enable the couplings to be dispensed with, had been under discussion at the same time as reconstruction of the pier. In April 1929 the Great Western wrote to the corporation:

> '. . . working over the tramway involves adjustment of the couplings of all trains conveying steamship passengers . . . and for some time past we have been considering methods of overcoming this difficulty'.

The letter enclosed plans for a new quay wall and infilling to carry a curve of greater radius, extending from St. Alban Street, through the Town Bridge, to St. Mary Street.

By the end of 1930, negotiations had reached the stage of a draft agreement but a number of contested details proved difficult to resolve and a year later little further progress had been made. Matters then drifted. In September 1935, in response to a corporation enquiry as to whether the company still wished to proceed, the question was reopened, but still another two years were to pass before all outstanding points were settled. An agreement between the corporation and the companies was eventually signed on 19th March 1938.

The agreement was supplemental to that of 1867 and since the work to be carried out involved a major deviation of the tramway itself (as distinct from the mere addition of sidings or minor realignment), the Weymouth & Portland, as owning company, was a party to it. The Great Western and the Southern (the latter as successor to the London & South Western) signed as leasing companies. Small variations of the basic scheme were incorporated in an amending agreement dated 1st July 1938. The more important was at the south end of Cosens's siding, where the original intention was to lift the old alignment and leave just a double siding, facing towards the station, with a combined dead-end for engine release but without direct access from the direction of the pier. This would have been inconvenient and by the July agreement through running over the old alignment was retained. The other alteration was opposite the end of St. Alban Street, where it had been intended to leave the old alignment intact; instead, a short length was cut out, resulting in a simpler layout.

When negotiations started, the Town Bridge that had figured in the construction of the tramway and in the 1888 alterations was in process of being replaced. At the north end, where the bridge approach intersects the tramway, the new bridge was designed to include two side arches, one over the existing line and the other over the water. In the light of the company's proposals, and at the company's expense, the 'water' arch was so designed and constructed that when the time came it could be utilised for the new alignment. Between St. Mary Street and Ferry's Corner the new wall was accordingly in line with the main pier of the bridge, the space behind being filled to carry the new curve. The company had hoped to retain the old alignment as well, as a loop, but the corporation stipulated its removal. The line of the new wall and the proposed and actual track plans are shown on Map No. 3, inset B.

Responsibility for the design and strength of the new wall rested with the leasing companies jointly but in practice the works were entirely a Great Western project, as we have seen, and they were carried out at Great Western expense. The agreement also placed on the companies the responsibility for maintaining the wall over the greater part of its length — i.e., to the extent that it was coextensive with their existing obligation in respect of the old wall (*Map No. 3, inset B*). That responsibility now devolves on the British Railways Board.

Work began, on either side of the Town Bridge, in March 1938, progressing towards the corner. From there northwards the reclamation was a more substantial undertaking, requiring the erection of a piled wooden staging along the line of the new wall from which the permanent piles could be driven. These were of reinforced concrete, and a pile yard, for their manufacture, was established in part of the goods yard, near Weymouth Junction. The new alignment under the bridge was opened for traffic at the beginning of March 1939 and the main curve the following July. The contractors were A. Jackaman & Son Ltd, of Slough.

The new curve has an average radius of about 6 chains and follows very closely the alignment of the viaduct shown on the deposited plan of 1861 (*Map No. 2, inset B*). Webb Major's (late Bagg's) siding and the original 'causeway' line of 1865 emerged as a single continuous loop, often referred to as the 'back road' or 'Cosens's', with Cosens's siding itself as a secondary loop. Although through running was possible, and occasionally resorted to, the loops were used in practice mainly as private sidings for neighbouring commercial premises.

As in the 1867 agreement, provision was made for the conveyance to the owning company — i.e., the Weymouth & Portland — of 'so much of the site and soil of the Backwater as is occupied by the Tramway' on the request of the leasing companies, but no conveyance has ever been made (under either agreement) and the formation, like the rest of the reclaimed area, remains corporation property.

The new curve enabled most carriage stock to use the tramway unhindered. Certain exceptions remained but these were less onerous than before — i.e., maximum length over buffers 64ft. 6in. (instead of 60ft. 6½in.) and maximum width over body 9ft. 3in. (or 66ft. 8in. over buffers by 8ft. 11in. over body). Authorised Great Western vehicles were marked WXQ by a small cast-iron plate at either end. Permanently close-coupled non-corridor sets were prohibited.

Although the special loose couplings were no longer to be

THE 1938/39 REALIGNMENT

Plate 28: The boat train negotiating Ferry's Corner in 1922, engine No. 1377; this view shows very clearly the extreme curvature of the original alignment. Note the caution board on the lamp post.

L.A. Wroot

Plates 29 & 30: Commercial Road in the vicinity of the new curve: (i) Shows the tramway (centre) and Webb Major's siding (formerly Bagg's) (right); (ii) About 100yds. lower down, showing the former marine coal siding (centre background), Webb Major's siding (right background), the tramway (foreground) and Cosens's siding (right).

L&GRP Collection, Courtesy David & Charles

Plate 31: The side arches of the Town Bridge as work was about to start, on 1st March 1938. Note the rough state of the roadway and the absence of check rails, as compared with *Plate 3*.

British Rail

Plates 32 & 33: Widening in progress: (i) August 1938, showing infilling on right while the train is still using the old alignment; (ii) March 1939, showing the new alignment completed at this point and the old alignment, (left) cut and awaiting lifting.

L&GRP Collection, Courtesy David & Charles

Plates 34-36: The main curve: (i) The temporary wooden staging along the line of the new wall, on 7th December 1938; (ii) The new wall complete and infilling in progress, on 7th March 1939; (iii) The new alignment complete, on 19th July 1939. Note the old alignment and Cosens's siding, right; also the permanent way hut, against Cosens's wall.

British Rail

Plate 37: Weymouth Quay plate, as displayed on permitted passenger vehicles. (Actual size, 5in. × 2½in.)
Courtesy Great Western Society

seen strewn in the 'six-foot' at Weymouth Junction between up and down boat train movements, a use was still found for one of them. During the flower season, in the early part of the year, it was customary to marshal the flower vans at the pier behind the passenger carriages. On leaving, the passenger train drew the vans forward to a more convenient position for loading and the long coupling, being easily slipped off by the shunter's pole, was a handy way of doing this. The practice lasted until 1959, when the boat trains were rerouted to Waterloo; with Buckeye-fitted Southern stock it was no longer practicable.

On the outbreak of war, the scheduled Channel Islands passenger service was immediately discontinued. A modified (night) service continued for a further week but without connecting trains; the last up train left the quay on Tuesday 5th September and the last down arrived at 2.20 the following morning. The tramway remained open for goods, and during May and June 1940 there was a temporary resumption of passenger working, when a number of specials were run to Paddington for refugees. Channel Islands cargo services continued until 1st July, when the islands were occupied by the Germans, and the final passenger train left the quay on 25th July, carrying survivors from the torpedoed French liner *Meknes*.

From 31st May 1940 the commercial pier was requisitioned and placed under naval control. More extensive requisitioning followed, including the cargo stage, near the eastern end of which a fence was erected across the quay, with gates for the tramway. One daily trip to the pier was still scheduled for military needs, though running only when required. Weymouth and Portland together were a major embarkation area for the invasion of Europe and an associated tramway development in 1943, during the run-up to the invasion, was a train ferry terminal, built by a port construction and repair group of the Royal Engineers and officially designated TFT 5. A cofferdam of steel sheet piling was built out from the quay wall at George Corner — the angle providing a convenient starting point — to a width of about 30ft. Filled with Portland spalls and capped with concrete, this then formed the base for a wooden pile pier, which curved round to run parallel with the quay wall as far as the west end of the cargo stage. A ferry berthed at the stage, which was strengthened for the purpose by three reinforced-concrete dolphins, would thus lie stern on to the pierhead. Work started in June 1943 and was completed early in 1944. The permanent way was laid and maintained on behalf of the War Department by the Great Western. The terminal was intended for the shipment of rolling stock to France in the wake of the invasion, using the Southern Railway's train ferries, but in the event it remained unused and as soon as the war was over it was removed. Demolition started in September 1945 and occupied just over a year. Unfortunately the terminal was not photographed officially and the only known photograph is that reproduced here. The plan on *page 42* is based on a drawing kindly supplied by the Commandmant of the former Royal Engineers Transportation Centre at Longmoor.

Plate 38: The train ferry terminal — a photograph taken during demolition, in 1946. The small craft moored alongside are an unfortunate intrusion but the bogie bolster wagon, standing on the pier while being loaded with piles that had formed the structure, shows the pier's position.
Author's Collection

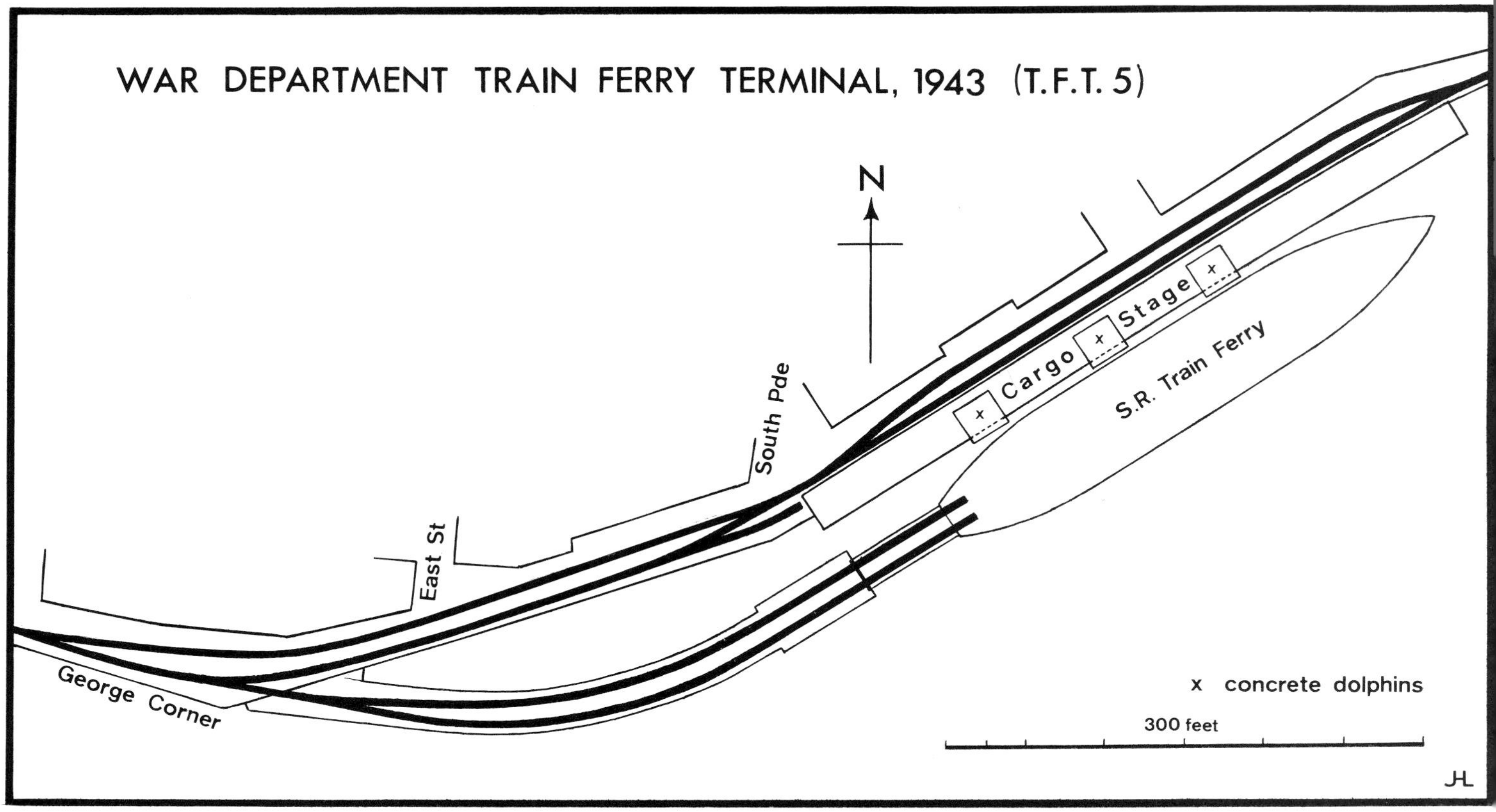

Normal commercial use of the tramway was resumed for goods in September 1945, as soon as the pier was de-requisitioned; the cargo stage was de-requisitioned a month later. Passenger trains began running again in June 1946. A general rehabilitation of the quay below the Town Bridge, held over because of the war, was even more necessary now, after wartime wear and tear. This applied both to the cargo stage and to the quay wall. The road and track, too, were in a very bad state of disrepair, with many sunken rail joints. Dust and noise were a constant cause of complaint, reminiscent of an earlier time.

A particular cause for concern was the quay wall along the length of Templeman's siding. In April 1947 the borough surveyor advised that having regard to the state of the wall the siding was unsafe. The Great Western responded by pointing out that it was essential for various firms' business as well as the railway's. Notwithstanding, they issued instructions prohibiting the siding to engines, and in April 1948, after a certain amount of discussion and correspondence, the corporation gave three months notice to terminate the 1882 agreement (as provided for in the agreement) but permitting the continued use of the siding for empty wagons only.

The cargo stage, already well past its prime in 1939, before its structural alteration as part of the train ferry terminal, was beyond redemption. In September 1948 a complete reconstruction was begun. This was completed in July 1951. Meanwhile, in May 1950, work was started on a new quay wall, extending from the west end of the cargo stage to St. Mary Street, where it joined the wall built by the Great Western in 1938. Over the length of the new wall the quay was widened by about 13ft., and during its construction both the tramway and Templeman's siding were subject to temporary slewing, so that the anchor beams and tie-bars could be positioned. On completion of the wall both tramway and siding were renewed, the work being carried

Plate 39: Custom House Quay and the old wooden cargo stage. This photograph was taken in 1938 but serves to show the condition of the track and roadway before the post-war reconstruction.
L&GRP Collection, Courtesy David & Charles

Plate 40: Relaying on Custom House Quay in February 1969, showing sleeperless track with chairs screwed to blocks set in concrete.

out during March and April 1952, and, on the application of the district civil engineer, rights of user in respect of the siding were restored in full (limited use having continued except when physically interrupted). Extensive relaying was undertaken at about the same time over the remaining length of the tramway, including check rails on those parts still without them. Between the stage and the Town Bridge the quay surface was concreted, to permit the use of caterpillar-tracked cranes, and the tramway chairs were screwed to greenheart blocks set into the concrete foundations instead of being laid on sleepers. On the completion of all these works the Railway Executive signed a twenty-year agreement with the corporation (17th June 1952) in respect of the new cargo stage, covering railway use of the berths and the installation of railway cranes.

A concurrent administrative change should not go unremarked. On 2nd April 1950 regional boundaries were redrawn. Operationally, for the time being, the tramway remained 'Western' but in all other respects, including the relaying last mentioned, it was now in the Southern Region — successor, one might say, to the London & South Western.

The predominant consideration affecting the Channel Islands service at this time was that all but two of the ships were overdue for replacement, most dating from as far back as 1925-6. Both routes, Southampton and Weymouth, were operating at a loss. At the end of 1957 orders were placed for four replacements, two passenger and two cargo, and, if the outlay on these was to be justified, rationalisation was inevitable — i.e., concentration of at least the passenger service on one port or the other. When all relevant factors were taken into account the balance of advantage was seen to lie with Weymouth, provided that corporation approval could be obtained for essential harbour works. Not for the first time there was a pronounced difference of outlook between 'port' and 'resort', the most contentious issue being the need for a third rail track on the pier. Uncertainty prevailed until February 1960 when, after a long debate, the town council voted by a narrow margin to meet the Transport Commission's requirements. The expected announcement followed in June: from the summer of 1961 the passenger service would be run by only three ships — the two new ones and the *St. Patrick* (1948) — and it would operate from Weymouth.

The works to be carried out were as follows:

Phase 1: provision of a third rail track and island platform on the pier, additional passing places on the tramway and new stores and offices on Custom House Quay (estimated cost £134,000);
Phase 2: replacement of single-storey buildings on the pier by two-storey, to create more space for the mechanised handling of cargo (estimated cost £77,000);
Phase 3: reclamation of land from the Backwater for a transit shed and sidings (estimated cost £206,000).

A formal agreement embodying part of the railway works scheduled under phase 1 and the new buildings (phase 2) was signed by the corporation and the Transport Commission on 20th February 1961. Meanwhile, in December, work had already started on the pier, it being essential to have the third track available by the start of the summer time table, the following May. In January the contractors were given full possession.

The additional width of pier that the corporation had agreed to make available was strictly limited, at one point to only 5ft. The third track could therefore be squeezed in only by reducing platform widths. The existing pier platform was cut back by about 6ft., permitting a corresponding slewing of Nos. 1 and 2 roads (*page 47, Plan A*), and the new island platform, between Nos. 2 and 3 roads, was limited to a width of 10ft. — 2ft. narrower than the old 'off-road' platform which it replaced. The original 1889 platform, which still survived as part of the pier platform, was of sub-standard height and had to be raised. The cut-back extended for 750ft., at which point the new and old platform faces converged.

Over the first 800ft. or so of its length the pier was solid, thus presenting no problem in the repositioning of the tracks and platforms, but the seaward end was of reinforced concrete piling and beams, dating from the 1932-3 reconstruction. The strength and cross section of that part was appropriate to the loading — i.e., the part that was under the rail tracks was at a lower level and of heavier

Plate 41: A general view of the pier as rebuilt in 1931-33, photographed on 30th September 1960, before the start of the 1961 improvements. The steamer is *St. Patrick* (1948).

Plate 42 (Left): The pier platform and baggage shed on 4th October 1960; note the dip in the platform level between the 1933 extension (nearer the camera) and the original platform of 1889. On the right is the 'off road' platform, dating from 1933.

Plate 43 (Right): Passengers crossing the tracks from the 'off road' platform, under the watchful eye of Chief Dock Foreman Ted Le Huray, on 13th June 1960. Note the barrier, to prevent accidental contact with greasy buffer heads.

THE 1961 WIDENING

Plate 44: This view, photographed on 6th January 1961, shows the cut-back of the pier platform.

Plate 45 (Right): 3rd February 1961: right — the new platform wall, with the pier road partly slewed; centre — the old alignment.

Plate 46 (Below): 23rd February 1961: left — the completed platform wall and the pier road slewed; centre — the 'off' road awaiting slewing; right — pre-cast components awaiting erection.

Plate 47: 6th April 1961: the switch diamond crossing being laid in, showing the slip connection between No. 2 road (centre) and No. 1 road (right, with wagons).

Plate 49 (Below Right): Before the new passenger ships entered service, each of them was open to inspection by the press and other invited guests. On 16th November 1960, passengers for the *Caesarea* travelled from Waterloo in first-class Pullmans *Juno, Alicante, Daphne, Cassandra* and *Niobe*, here seen on Custom House Quay behind No. 1367; the new bucket was drawn from stores specially for the occasion. Guests lunched on board while the ship cruised up-channel to Southampton. Apart from an enthusiasts' excursion, in 1956, this was the first appearance of Pullmans on the tramway.

Plate 48 (Below): 7th May 1961, the works nearing completion; the pier road and platform in use and the new island platform awaiting surfacing. The vessel unloading tomatoes is the *Elk* (1959).

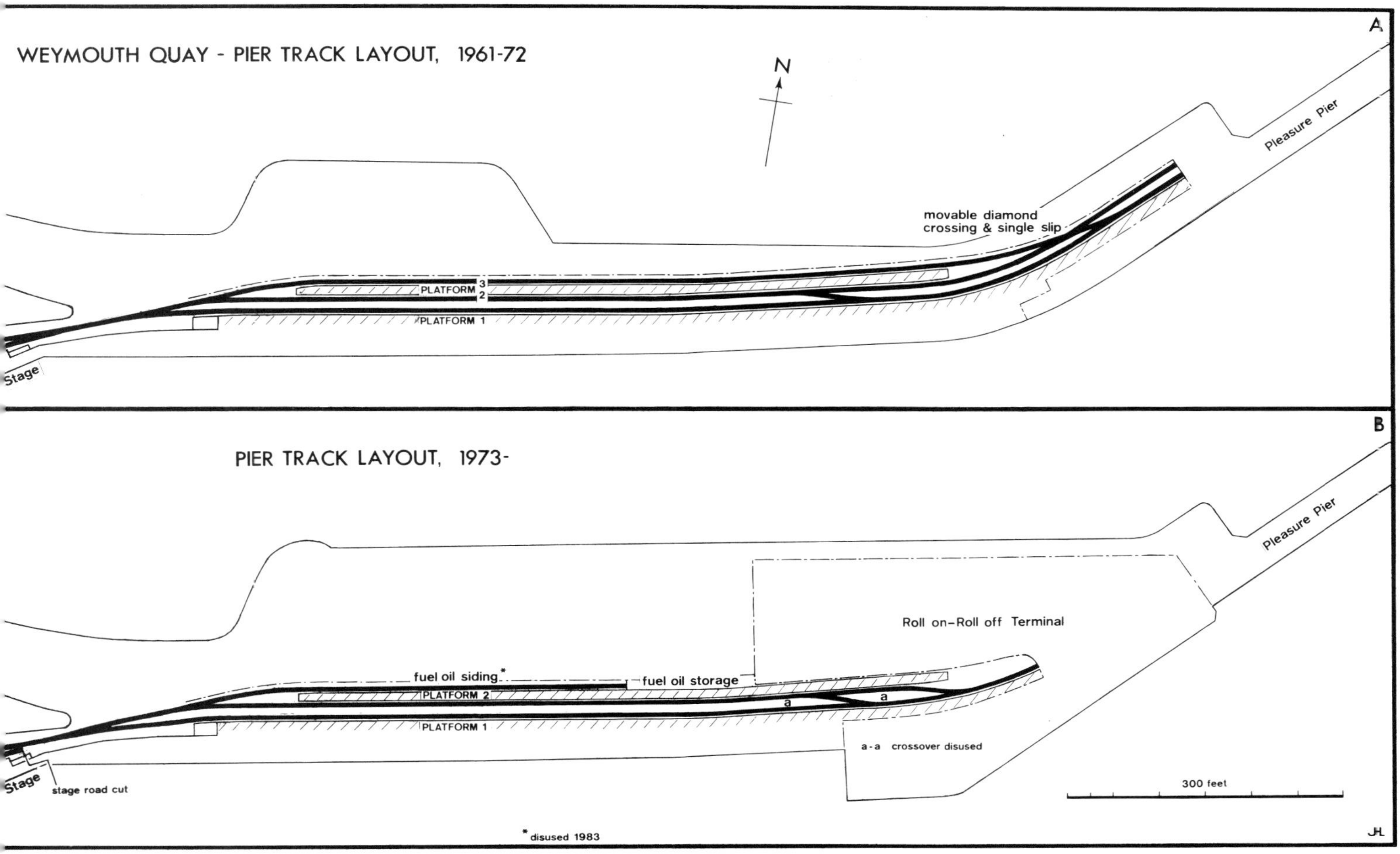
A
WEYMOUTH QUAY - PIER TRACK LAYOUT, 1961-72
N
Pleasure Pier
movable diamond
crossing & single slip
PLATFORM 3
2
PLATFORM 1
Stage
B
PIER TRACK LAYOUT, 1973-
Pleasure Pier
Roll on-Roll off Terminal
fuel oil siding*
fuel oil storage
PLATFORM 2
a
a
PLATFORM 1
a-a crossover disused
Stage
stage road cut
300 feet
*disused 1983
JHL

CAFE

Plate 50: The *Sarnia's* introductory cruise, on 13th June 1961, was in the opposite direction, passengers embarking at Southampton and then returning to Waterloo by Pullman from Weymouth. The train, consisting of cars *Juno, Joan, Cassandra, Octavia* and *Aurora*, is seen at Westham crossing behind No. 9756.

Plate 51 (Below): Following correspondence between the author and Southern Region, the first day of the reorganised service was marked by the reintroduction of CHANNEL ISLANDS BOAT EXPRESS roof boards, formerly associated with the Paddington trains; the Southern boards carried the additional wording WATERLOO — WEYMOUTH. The train is here seen running into No. 1 platform on the first day of the new timetable, 13th May 1961.

construction than the rest. The convergence of the new track (No. 3 road) with Nos. 2 and 1 was 130ft. beyond the end of the solid part, necessitating extensive reconstruction and strengthening.

What was possibly the most interesting feature of the new layout was the junction of No. 3 road with Nos. 2 and 1. Direct connection between Nos. 3 and 2 was impossible, because of the lack of space. The existing crossover between Nos. 1 and 2 was therefore run on to the end of No. 3, with a diamond crossing at the intersection with No. 2, connection between Nos. 1 and 2 being preserved by the provision of a slip road. As the angle and the restricted space precluded the fitting of check rails a standard diamond crossing could not be used. The alternative was a specially designed crossing with movable switches. A switch diamond would not normally be used in a location calling for slip rails as well and the combination is thought to have been unique. The movements to be catered for required the diamond to be operated independently of the slip road — even supposing that the complexities of combined operation could have been overcome — and two separate levers gave the shunters one or two problems until they got used to the idea. Minor derailments were not unknown but with care the crossing gave little trouble. It was intended to be used solely for engine release but wagons were also shunted over it on occasion.

All the trackwork and the new platforms were finished in time for the 1961 summer timetable, and this stage of the work was completed by the installation of a new fuel-oil pipeline system and the demolition of some pier buildings.

Work on the tramway was resumed during the winter. In January and February 1962 new sidings were laid down by the Backwater, between the new and old alignments (*page 52 Plan B*), and the track under the Town Bridge was relaid. A weekend occupation for laying in the turnouts for the sidings produced the rare sight — in modern times — of a train running over the old alignment. By the early fifties use of the 'back road' as a private siding had virtually died out, and since the 1938 agreement specifically precluded wagons from standing there for any other purpose — i.e., its use as an ordinary traffic siding — it then became more or less redundant. Cosens's siding was lifted in November 1957, and a gangers' hut which had stood nearby since 1902 was removed at about the same time.

Plate 52: No. 1368 running through the 'back road' — i.e., the original alignment of 1865 — with an early morning flower train during construction of the new Backwater sidings, Sunday, 14th January 1962.

Plate 53: The new Backwater sidings under construction, on 22nd January 1962. The notice board was a warning not to park within 6ft. of any railway line.

The relaying under the Town Bridge was designed to alleviate the problem of flooding and delay to traffic at certain tides. With the consent of the Ministry of Transport to a reduction in overhead clearance from 6in. to 4in., and the acceptance of a maximum vehicle height of 13ft. 1in. (in practice of little consequence), it was possible to raise the rail level by 6½in. The relaid length was Thermit-welded. In view of the restriction on vehicle height, the tramway load gauge at Weymouth Junction was modified to correspond. It is interesting to recall that in 1937 when the Ferry's Corner agreement was being negotiated, the corporation suggested that the Great Western might wish, in their own interest, to do something about the flooding problem at the same time. They declined.

Plate 54: Track renewal under the Town Bridge, on 31st January 1962. The old track has been exposed, by removal of the concrete roadway, and is awaiting lifting. The low angle shows the dip very clearly.

Plates 55 & 56: Raising the track under the Town Bridge eased the flooding problem but did not cure it, although fortunately the Weymouth tidal constants are such that the highest tides occur at times when interference with traffic is least likely. (i) No. D2397 about to pass under the bridge with the track covered to a depth of about 3in., on 15th October 1966. Note the flood mark on the bridge pier. (ii) No. 33029 negotiating rather deeper water en route to the quay with fuel oil, on 7th September 1979. Locomotives of Class 33 are permitted by the current tramway instructions to pass through up to 6in. of flood water (as indicated by the flood mark) subject to examination afterwards by Chief Mechanical & Electrical Engineer's staff.

(i) *C.L. Caddy*
(ii) *P. Henshaw*

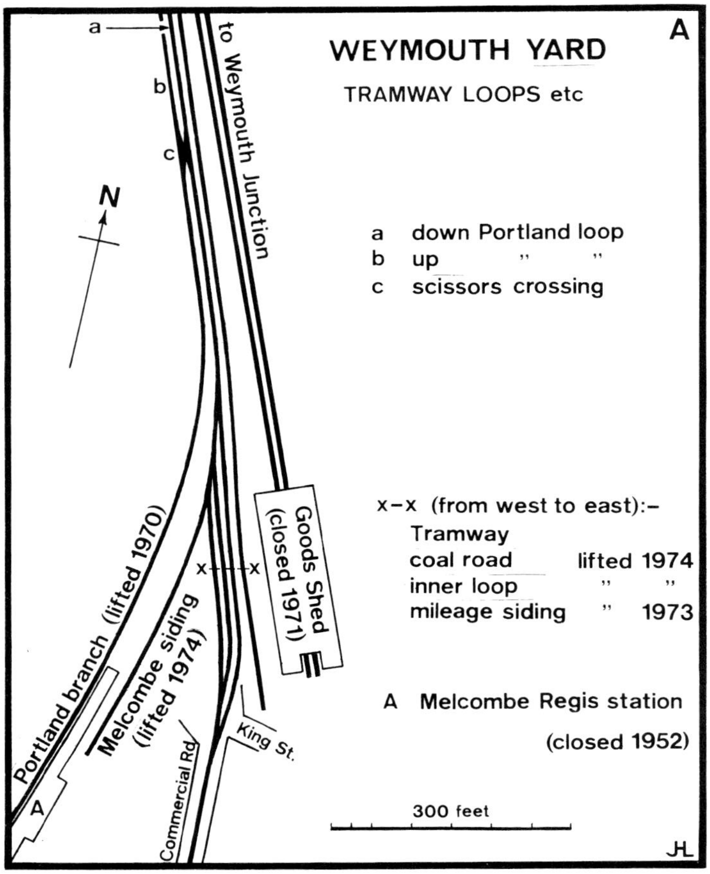

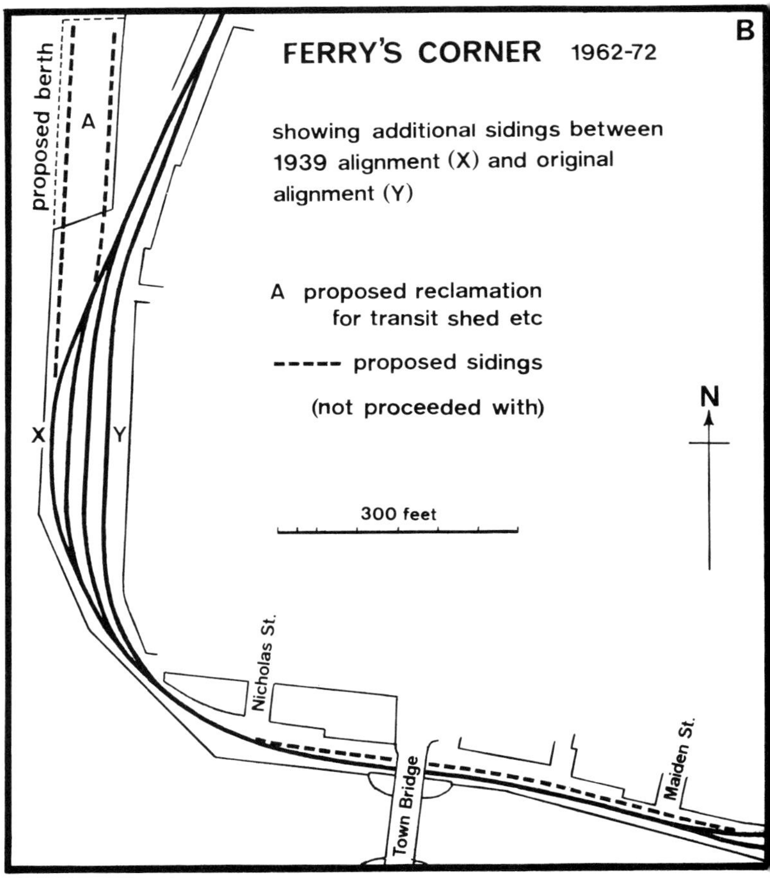

The new works were inspected for the Ministry of Transport on 11th October 1962 by Col. Robertson. The 1939 curve, incidentally, had by then been used by passenger trains for more than sixteen years without inspection, as the inspection that would have been made was cancelled because of the war.

Because of 'financial stringency', the rest of the new building programme covered by phase 2 was carried out piecemeal, and was not completed until 1967. The rest of phase 1, comprising the stores etc., proposed to be built on Custom House Quay and a tramway loop extending westwards from Maiden Street through the inner arch of the Town Bridge as far as Nicholas Street, and the whole of phase 3, were abandoned. As regards phase 3, berths near the station, with access through a new bridge with a lifting span (as built in 1930) had been suggested as far back as 1923, as a means of ending what an official report of that date referred to as the 'vexatious and uncomfortable crawl through the streets'. In principle, the idea of Backwater berths was thus not new but its resurrection as late as 1960 was unrealistic, and abandonment not surprising.

With concentration of the service on Weymouth, the summer passenger traffic on the tramway reached a new peak. The increase was most conspicuous on Saturday afternoons, when two incoming steamers disembarked anything up to 2,500 passengers, requiring five boat trains. Four of these were berthed at the pier together — an unprecendented sight — stock for the fifth being brought down as platform space was vacated by earlier departures. On Fridays and Saturdays two trains, and sometimes a third, were run from Waterloo to connect with night sailings.

Regrettably, results did not fully match prediction, and the peak was short-lived. As part of a cost-cutting contraction that followed, the number of trains was reduced. After November 1962 the winter boat trains were run only if required — in practice, seldom.

Potentially more serious for the future of the tramway was a marked drop in some important freight traffics and the growing tendency for freight generally to travel by road, following the pattern so depressingly familiar in the rail freight field at large.

This began in 1955, during the three-week strike by the drivers' union, ASLEF. Some traffic diverted then never returned to rail, and the process continued. In 1965, check rails were laid throughout on Nos. 1 and 2 roads on the pier (instead of only half way as before), the surface then being filled in to rail level, to facilitate access by lorries. A particularly serious blow in 1964 was the loss of half the Guernsey tomato traffic to the Guernsey-based Commodore Shipping Company, running into Shoreham. Bad rail transits to certain markets threw much of what was left to the road hauliers. The last of the 'Perpots' — the special trains for perishables and potatoes that were once such a feature of Weymouth's freight working — ran in 1970. The following year the introduction of the few still scheduled was postponed because of threatened industrial action (unrelated to Weymouth), and the postponement became permanent.

The overriding trend during the late sixties, however, was the move towards 'unit loading' — i.e., the complete containerisation of all cargo. A decision to apply this principle to Channel Islands freight, concentrating on only one mainland port, was announced towards the end of 1969, after protracted investigation. In theory the port had yet to be decided, but for Weymouth to provide the necessary space for large numbers of ISO containers and the special cranes needed to handle them was not a realistic option. Thus it proved. Withdrawal of all freight shipments through Weymouth was announced in February 1971, in favour of a joint British Rail/Commodore operation to be

Plates 57-59: Swan song — Saturday boat trains standing at the pier during the 1960s (i) 8th July 1961; (ii) 4th August 1962 (*compare with Plate 41*); (iii) 4th July 1964.

Plate 60: Saturday afternoon blackboards. The left-hand board sets out the scheduled departures; the right-hand was mainly for the benefit of passengers arriving by the second boat, which was often late, thus failing to connect with the 4.15 train.

based on Portsmouth. The last rail freight, in and out, was handled on 28th February 1972 and from 1st March the service was formally withdrawn. The Portsmouth operation started the following October, after an interim period during which traffic continued to pass through Southampton. Except for the passenger trains and fuel oil for the steamers, the tramway was now redundant.

THE TRAFFIC THAT HAS GONE

Plate 61: Spring flowers, an important passenger-rated traffic seen in this view dated 12th March 1959.

Plate 62: Jersey potatoes at the stage, on 28th May 1959.

Plates 63 & 64: Guernsey tomatoes: (i) In chips, on 24th May 1959 – perhaps up to 70,000 in a cargo, every one man-handled in the ship's hold and again into wagons; (ii) In trays, on 9th June 1962, palletised for mechanical handling. In 1962 (after limited use the previous season) a fleet of upwards of 300 designated 'Palvans' was introduced to give faster transits, but their unfortunate tendency to derail at speeds above 45 m.p.h. led two years later to their replacement by 'Vanwides' (vans with a pair of sliding doors, giving a wide central opening).

Plate 65: Jersey broccoli, on 3rd March 1960, reminiscent of the French cargoes of thirty years earlier.

Plate 66: A typical pier scene of the 1960s, photographed on 28th May 1961, with all three roads full of box vans. Note the goods brake, a type of vehicle only occasionally seen on the tramway. It was also unusual to see a pannier 'bunker up' (in this case No. 9620). 'Chimney up' was in accordance with very long standing practice dictated by driving convenience when shunting the yard. The diesels and 2-6-2Ts, for the same reason, and again with only rare exceptions, faced the other way.

CHAPTER TEN

The Tram Engines

In the present context, the term 'tram engine', although not incorrect, may still give a misleading impression, for the conventional tram engine, with wheels fenced in, was a type that the Great Western never possessed. Perhaps fortunately for the company, when councillors were considering allowing the use of an engine on the tramway their concern seems to have been not so much to guard against accident as to ensure that if one occurred the corporation would not be blamed. Nobody called for the engine to be fitted with side screens, though the anti-tramway faction would surely have done so had they thought of it. The possibility of engines having to be built specifically for the tramway thus never arose, and a hundred years later it is a matter of historical record that no accident has ever occurred on the line that screens would have prevented.

As it was, many years elapsed before any Great Western-built engine appeared. What the instructions referred to with a fine pretension as 'engines of a special class' were merely such oddments as were available and suitable, their only common feature apart from small size and light weight being 'foreign' origin — all came into Great Western stock with the take-over of other companies. It was, of course, the sharp curvature and the state of the quay wall that precluded all but the smallest and lightest, and once chosen some stayed for a very long time. Diversity adds to their interest.

Contemporary accounts unfortunately do not identify the engine sent on trial in 1878 and put into service in 1880 but the evidence points to its having been No. 2, a small 2-4-0 side tank built in 1871 for the broad gauge Torbay & Brixham Railway. It was then named *King. King* came into Great Western ownership in 1876, via the South Devon Railway, when the companies amalgamated, and in March 1878 was converted at Swindon to standard gauge. That it emerged from Swindon, as No. 2, just at the time of the trial, may have been no more than coincidence, but assuming the weight quoted by the *County Chronicle* to have been correct this must have been the engine sent to Weymouth. The Great Western had no other weighing as little as 12 tons 5cwt. or 'one ton less than a loaded truck'. There is no record of its exact weight in 1878 but a later diagram, issued after the fitting of larger tanks, quoted a figure of 13 tons 17cwt. If allowance is made for the increased water capacity, 12 tons 5cwt. is about right. We also have it on the evidence of a retired driver of the author's acquaintance many years ago, who joined the Great Western at Weymouth in 1896, when 'the first engine on the tramway' was well within memory, that it was No. 2. It is, in fact, very probable that the engine's conversion to standard gauge as early as 1878 was with the tramway in mind.

No. 2 was probably a little small even for the tramway but a pair of engines that proved to be ideal were Nos. 1376 and 1377. Built in the Bristol & Exeter Railway shops at Bristol to work the Culm Valley Light Railway, they were 0-6-0 side tanks and, like No. 2, passed to the Great Western under the 1876 amalgamation. In 1881 both were extensively rebuilt at Swindon and soon afterwards were transferred to Weymouth; it is with Weymouth that they will always be associated. The first definite Weymouth reference is dated 2nd January 1886, when No. 1377 ran away while towing 'a large goods engine' off shed and finished up in the station, doing considerable damage to itself and other rolling stock, but it is likely that by then both had been at Weymouth for some time. For more than forty years the tramway depended on these two engines above all others. No. 1377, incidentally, was in trouble again in 1903 when it ran through open trap points at the George Corner and was stopped within inches of going over the harbour wall.

Plate 67: No. 2, from a water colour by P.J.T. Reed. This shows the engine as it was after the fitting of larger tanks and as an illustration of the engine sent to Weymouth is therefore only approximately correct. Also, being based on a diagram, it is to some extent conjectural, although comparison with a recently discovered photograph of the engine on the Lambourn line reveals remarkably little disparity — most noticeably a non-tapering chimney and that the cab, instead of being full width, had the front and back plates cut away.

Author's Collection

Plate 68: No. 1376, photographed on the tramway just inside the yard gates with a group of tramway staff, circa 1906. From left to right: George Vowles, tramway flagman; John Gill, tramway inspector; Jack Travers, goods inspector, tramway; and the engine crew (not identified).

Author's Collection

Plate 69: No. 1377 running light at the George Corner, circa 1924. Note the shunter, riding seated.

Seward, Weymouth

Plate 70: No. 1376 passing Alexandra Terrace with the 'up' boat train in 1921. The gardens on the right, on land reclaimed from the Backwater (*see Plates 13 and 14*), have now in turn disappeared, in part, to make way for a traffic roundabout. Note the 'hook' shunter's step and rail hand-hold — although in this case the shunter prefers to ride on the cab step.

R. Brookman

Plate 71: A pre-1914 view of the boat train passing Alexandra Terrace, behind one of the Bristol & Exeter tanks. It makes an interesting comparison with *Plate 13,* which shows the same location photographed from the opposite direction, and also with *Plates 84 and 87.*

Seward, Weymouth, Courtesy Photomatic Ltd.

Plate 72: No. 1376 about to back on to the boat train, on 20th May 1902. In the background, the steamer *Reindeer* is just coming alongside from the Channel Islands, watched by the usual little groups of interested onlookers.

J.B. Sherlock

Among the engines that worked on the tramway during the reign of the Bristol & Exeter tanks the best-known were *Fox* (No. 1391), built for the West Cornwall Railway and taken into Great Western stock in 1876, and *Hook Norton* (No. 1337), bought in 1904 from the liquidators of an Oxfordshire industrial concern, the Hook Norton Ironstone Partnership. In 1904 the Bristol divisional superintendent raised the question of more powerful engines but the divisional engineer demurred:

> The engine at present working on the Tramway has a total weight of 22t 6c spread over three pairs of wheels coupled and this I consider is the maximum weight that should go over the Tramway. The Quay Walls were never constructed to carry heavy weights . . . Why cannot the trains when very heavy be taken by two small engines?

His suggestion was put to the divisional locomotive superintendent, who looked carefully into the matter and gave instructions that whenever there was a heavy train it was to be worked 'by one of the usual tram engines assisted by the *Fox*' which would, he thought, 'get over the difficulty'. Whether *Fox* ever did assist in this way history does not record. Perhaps there is a photograph somewhere, waiting to be discovered. *Hook Norton* left Weymouth in 1907 on being sold to the Fishguard & Rosslare Railways & Harbours Company, but in 1913 it returned to Great Western stock and soon afterwards was back on the tramway. Despite the 1888-89 renewal of the quay wall, Templeman's siding remained subject to a weight limit of 18 tons, making *Fox* the only engine permitted to run over it.

The several hundred locomotives taken into Great Western stock as a result of the Grouping included another

Plates 73 & 74: There is no known photograph of *Fox* actually working on the tramway. In the first of these two views the engine is standing on the engine road, at the approach to Weymouth shed, and in the second at the back of the shed, with the running lines in the background, beyond the spike fence.

(i) *Seward, Weymouth*
(ii) *Author's Collection*

Plate 75: A classic tramway 'portrait' of *Hook Norton*, standing just inside the yard gates about 1906. Note the tow-rope (over the smokebox door handles) and the trunnion-mounted bell; also the 'broad gauge' track, consisting of bridge rail on longitudinal timbers, more than thirty years after the gauge conversion. The right-hand figure is once again Inspector John Gill who, it must be said, had a knack of being around whenever there was a camera about.

Seward, Weymouth

Plate 76: The driver of *Hook Norton* takes his ease while awaiting 'right away' to take the boat train to Weymouth Junction, circa 1922. Note the bracket-mounted bell.

Author's Collection

Plate 77: No. 1386 passing the George Inn with goods in October 1909. Note the open doors on empty wagons. The steamer is the Hain Line vessel *Trevanion*, from the Sea of Azov with Russian barley — a good example of the non-railway cargoes which provided additional traffic for the tramway.

Seward, Weymouth

pair that were to become very familiar on the tramway, Nos. 2194 and 2195, *Kidwelly* and *Cwm Mawr*, lately of the Burry Port & Gwendraeth Valley Railway. After a long spell at Swindon both arrived at Weymouth in 1926, *Kidwelly* about March or April (replacing *Hook Norton*, withdrawn and cut up in January that year) and *Cwm Mawr* about September. On the arrival of *Cwm Mawr*, No. 1377 appears to have stopped work on the tramway as photographs taken towards the end of the year show the engine without its bell, but it remained at Weymouth until withdrawn from service in January 1927. The other Bristol & Exeter tank, No. 1376, worked with *Kidwelly* and *Cwm Mawr* until 1928, when it was found fresh employment at Oswestry. As a replacement, Weymouth received No. 1331. Taken

Plate 78: No. 2195,*Cwm Mawr*, passing along Custom House Quay with the 'up' boat train, circa 1929. Note the shunter's step, rail hand-hold, tow-rope and stirrup-mounted bell; also the wooden steps lying in the roadway and side lamps on the leading carriage.

Author's Collection

Plate 79: No. 2194, *Kidwelly*, with the 'up' boat train, passing through the inner arch of the Town Bridge in 1933.

H.N. Shepherd, Courtesy I.D. Beale

Plate 80 (Above): Against the backdrop of Weymouth's sands *Kidwelly* stands at the pier with a single carriage, circa 1934. The reason for the shunting movement is not known but it was not uncommon for a certain amount of remarshalling of the boat train(s) to take place at the pier. Note the screw and loose couplings at the rear end of the carriage.
Seward, Weymouth

Plate 81 (Above): A similar view, this time with *Cwm Mawr.* Note the Ocean Mails van, a type of vehicle regularly included in pre-1939 boat trains.
Seward, Weymouth

Plate 82: Long a commonplace, now but a memory — goods being shunted at the pier, on 16th August 1938. The engine is *Kidwelly.*

into Great Western stock from the Whitland & Cardigan Railway in 1886, as No. 1387, this engine was in 1902 transferred to departmental stock, only to be returned to capital stock, after rebuilding, in 1927, by which time it was fifty years old. It served at Weymouth from 1928 until October 1935. Interestingly, for two months in 1931 while No. 1331 was under repair at Bristol, the engine that replaced it at Weymouth was once again No. 1376.

Particulars of the engines so far mentioned, and of others that worked on the tramway between 1880 and 1935, are shown in Table I. All the regular tramway engines are included but it is impossible to list the many that have relieved at various times. These were often of the 1392 Class (ex Cornwall Minerals Railway) but perhaps the most interesting was London & North Western 0-4-0 saddle tank No. 3033, reported on the tramway in June 1917. Apart from the three side tanks already mentioned (Nos. 2, 1376 and 1377) and *Fox* (0-4-0 saddle tank) all those listed were 0-6-0 saddle tanks.

Plate 83: In the early part of 1929, while *Kidwelly* was in Swindon, its place on the tramway was taken by No. 679, here seen running up Commercial Road with a mixed load. The third wagon is the pump wagon (*see Plate 149*) sandwiched between oil tank wagons. The front step and hand-hold were transferred temporarily from *Kidwelly*.

Author's Collection

Plate 84: The 'up' boat train crossing the end of King Street behind No. 1331, in 1933. The shunter is just mounting the front step to ride to the junction after ensuring 'all clear' as regards road traffic.

H.N. Shepherd, Courtesy I.D. Beale

Table I
Weymouth Tramway Engines 1878 – 1946 (*see also Table II*)

	Engine	*Built*	*Origin*	*Weight Total* t c	*Max. Axle* t c	*Tramway Service*
2		AE, 1871	SDR	13 17	4 16	1878, 1880–?
1376		B&E, 1874	B&E	22 6	7 12	by 1886–1928, 1931
1377		B&E, 1875				by 1886–c. Dec. 1926
1391	*Fox*	AE, 1872	WCR	18 0	11 8	Apr. 1903–May 1906, Mar.–Oct. 1908
1337	*Hook Norton*	MW, 1889	HNIP	23 12	8 7	Nov. 1904–1907, Jan. 1914–Jan. 1926
1386		FW, 1875	W&C	24 13	9 0	May 1909–Mar. 1911
2194	*Kidwelly*	AE, 1903	BPGV	32 1	11 1	c. Apr. 1926–1940
2195	*Cwm Mawr*	AE, 1905				c. Sep. 1926–Mar. 1939, Nov. 1945–Jun. 1946
1331		FW, 1877	W&C	31 12	10 16	1928–Oct. 1935
679		Pkt, 1890	ADR	26 17	10 8	c. Jan.–Jun. 1929
1397		SS, 1873	CMR	30 16	10 17	Jun.–Jul. 1931

AE Avonside Engine Co.
B&E Bristol & Exeter Railway
MW Manning Wardle
FW Fox Walker
Pkt Peckett
SS Sharp Stewart
SDR South Devon Railway
WCR West Cornwall Railway.
HNIP Hook Norton Ironstone Partnership
W&C Whitland & Cardigan Railway
BPGV Burry Port & Gwendraeth Valley Railway
ADR Alexandra Docks & Railway
CMR Cornwall Minerals Railway

The first standard Great Western engine to appear on the tramway — except possibly for the occasional use of the 1361 class as relief — was 1366 class pannier tank No. 1367, which arrived from Swindon early in 1935. In March 1939 *Cwm Mawr* was withdrawn and replaced by a second pannier, No. 1371; *Kidwelly* stayed until 1940. Like many other engines withdrawn at that time, however, *Cwm Mawr* was not scrapped but later reinstated, to help the war effort, and in 1945 (as plain No. 2195) returned for a while to the tramway.

Somewhat surprisingly the working instructions did not specify permitted classes until 1947. Those then listed were the 1366 and 74XX classes and No. 1331 (also described as a 'class'). In practice the line was then worked almost entirely by the 1366 class. No. 1331 had long since left and did not return and the 74XX were represented at Weymouth by only one engine (7408). The three 1366s that were available were adequate for all normal tramway duties and the men preferred them, dismissing the 74XX as 'too high in the wheel'. It is not known when that class was first used; the first recorded use was of No. 7418, in July 1951, but certainly until 1953 they were used only infrequently.

Plate 85: No. 7418 alongside the cargo stage — a quiet moment in 1953, shortly after the reconstruction of the stage but before the installation of the cranes.
K. Bannister

Plate 86: No. 7421 on the 'up' boat train at Ferry's Corner, circa 1953. Note the position of the headlamp.

K. Bannister

Plate 87: The boat train crossing the end of King Street headed by No. 7408 on 19th August 1954, while shunters stand at either side to control road traffic. The name of the public house on the corner is not without relevance.

M. Hale

In 1953, however, further members of the class were transferred to Weymouth and unexpectedly took over. The reason was that although the new quay wall had been designed to meet loading criteria laid down by the Railway Executive these were based on the 5700 class (added to the list of permitted classes in January 1951) — i.e., a total weight not exceeding 47½ tons spread over three axles and a wheelbase of at least 15ft. 6in. After a time, somebody seems to have realised that, interpreted strictly, the resultant loading of approximately 3.1 tons per foot precluded the 1366 class which, though lighter, had a wheelbase of only 11ft., giving a corresponding figure of 3¼ tons.

Concern was not so much for the tramway itself as for Templeman's siding, which was 'nearer the edge'. In March 1953, on the application of the district civil engineer, permission was given for the 1366s to run over the siding. In practice the wall had, of course, been built to withstand loads well in excess of the specified figures, probably at least double. Inevitably it took time for the change to be given effect and in the meantime the engines had gone elsewhere. Two returned in September 1953 but the third did not do so until the end of 1954. On 22nd December 1954 a fresh agreement was signed in respect of the siding, covering its maintenance by the Transport Commission and authorising a loading of 3¼ tons per foot, with a maximum axle loading of 20 tons.

Although permitted from 1951 the 5700 class were not used on the tramway regularly until about 1956. The slightly heavier 8750 class did not appear until May 1960 when, to meet a temporary shortage of permitted classes, the necessary relaxation was authorised. Thereafter the two versions of 'large pannier' were regarded as one for tramway purposes, working alongside the 1366s — but never superseding them. From 1946 until diesels took over the only 'non-panniers' to be seen were Nos. 1363 (1949) and 1361 (1960) of the 1361 class.

Although perhaps better known for their work on the tramway, the 1366s were built primarily for works shunting at Swindon, which was where the other members of the class spent most of their time. By 1948 all had spent some time at Weymouth with the exception of No. 1369, which remained at Swindon until March 1960. Then, its arrival on the tramway struck a faintly nostalgic note. On the tanks, just discernible through the discolouration of twenty-six years as a works shunter, was still the old and honoured name, GREAT WESTERN.

In October 1960 Weymouth shed received its first diesel

Plate 88: The boat train, of three carriages, berthed at the pier on 2nd January 1958. This was the normal winter formation at the time, the quay carriages being combined at the junction with the 4.10p.m. from the town station — a practice begun in 1889 and varied only for a brief period before the 1939 war, when a separate boat train was run in winter as in summer.

Plate 89: In this unusual view, photographed on 6th March 1958, the train is berthed at the cargo stage, the pier road being fully occupied by vans for the spring flower traffic. Passengers on such occasions had to walk the short distance from the steamer to the cargo stage.

Plate 90: No. 1368 on Custom House Quay with a perishables train, in June 1955.

Plate 91: No. 1367 shunting at the pier, on 12th November 1956.

Plate 92: No. 1369 shunting at the cargo stage on 30th March 1960, while broccoli awaits removal by competing road transport. Note the absence of the shunter's step and hand-hold, and of steam heat. Although steam heat was fitted later, No. 1369 did not receive a step or hand-hold.

Plate 93: No. 1369 at Westham crossing, on 7th April 1960.

Plate 94 (Above): Two are sometimes better than one. It was rare to see two tram engines double-heading, but after being stopped by road vehicles parked foul of the track the train engine sometimes had difficulty in restarting and on occasion, when a second engine was available at the pier, it was sent to assist. In this case, on 22nd June 1960, No. 1367 has gone to the assistance of No. 1368.

Plate 95 (Above): The last day of tramway service for the 1366 class. No. 1367, the 'oldest inhabitant', with continuous service from 1935, (except for the brief interregnum in 1953) bringing in the boat train while No. 1369, the last to arrive, stands on No. 2 road with goods, on 12th June 1962.

Plate 96 (Right): On one of the first appearances on the tramway of the large panniers, 27th June 1956, No. 5784 stands with the boat train on the 'off road' (later No. 2).

Plate 97: During the 1960s, there was a brief resumption of large-scale broccoli imports from France, at one time an important tramway traffic. The crates stacked high on either side of the line in this view (18th April 1963) may be compared with *Plates 24 and 25*, but there, unfortunately, the similarity ends for these cargoes were transported entirely by road.

Plate 98: Despite the similarity of the 1361 and 1366 classes their paths seldom crossed, and the tramway was probably the only place where they could be seen working together. Nos. 1361 and 1367 are here seen at the pier on 22nd March 1960.

Plates 99 & 100: Two further views of No. 1361 during its brief appearance on the tramway in 1960: (i) Shunting goods on 2nd February; the step and hand-hold are the same as those fitted to the 1366 class; (ii) On the boat train, on 15th February.

shunter, No. D2292 (204hp diesel-mechanical), and a tramway trial inevitably followed. It took place on 7th April 1961 but the regular use of diesels was delayed until the following year by a manning dispute. A union demand for double manning, not unreasonable in view of the peculiar difficulties of working on the public roads in modern traffic conditions, was eventually conceded. No. D2292 was first used on normal tramway duty on 9th February 1962, remaining on the quay for the next three or four days to shunt while the pier was temporarily isolated by the Town Bridge relaying. It hauled the boat train for the first time on 14th February. As others of the class arrived, steam was gradually displaced. No. 1368 left in April 1962. Nos. 1367 and 1369 worked on the tramway together for the last time on 12th June and on the 23rd left Weymouth behind No. 31798, dead, bound for the Western Region. The last 57XX (7782) and various 8750s continued to appear at intervals for a further eighteen months, prolonging the period of transition, during which old and new worked side by side, to nearly two years. The last Great Western engine to run on the tramway was No. 4610, which hauled the up boat train on Christmas Eve 1963.

Plates 101 & 102: The beginning of the diesel era — Drewry 204hp shunter No. D2292 on 9th February 1962, the first appearance of one of these engines on the tramway in ordinary service: (i) Shunting at the pier; (ii) Shunters Alan Bown and Brian Hook climbing aboard after halting road traffic at Westham crossing.

Plate 103 (Below): Transition: steam and diesel together on 16th February 1962, a scene to be repeated, with variations, more or less regularly for the next couple of years. Note the small bell on No. 1368; this turned up on various engines from time to time.

Plate 104: The two versions of 204hp shunter — Nos. D2295 (Drewry) and D2397 (BR), standing on Custom House Quay on 20th May 1964.

Plate 105: A solo of No. D2398 (BR) standing on No. 2 road at the pier on 14th June 1962.

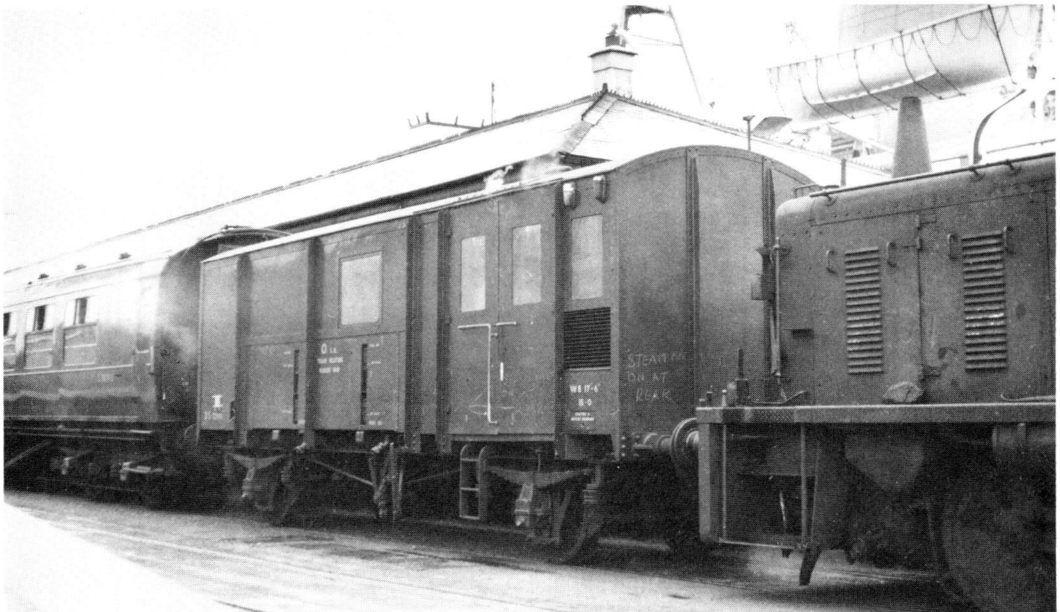

Plate 106: Boiler van No. DS70191 marshalled at the head of the boat train on 20th January 1964.

A consequence of the disappearance of steam was the introduction of boiler vans for use with the winter boat trains. Two were built at Ashford in 1963 (DS 70190/1). By the time they were available, however, the decision to run an up winter boat train only when it was required had already been taken and their work on the tramway was limited to perhaps half a dozen appearances, mainly during the winter of 1963-4. The last recorded use of a van (DS 70191) was on 28th December 1964, an unscheduled working to cater for the return Christmas peak. They were in any case not to be relied on. The final appearance of a pannier on the tramway, just mentioned, had about it an air of tragicomedy. A diesel was rostered but no boiler van was available; No. 4610 – presumably the only alternative – had lost its rear steam-heating connection; it was therefore specially turned, only for the shunters to discover, at the quay, that the front connection was also unusable, because the cock had jammed.

Plates 107 & 108: The first appearance of LMS Class 2P on the tramway, on Saturday, 4th July 1964: (i) No. 41261 heading for the junction with assorted vans, escorted by shunters Dave Mercer and Ray Dunn — note the Class A headlamps; (ii) With a relief boat train at No. 3 platform.

Plate 109: No. 41298 about to depart with the 'up' boat train on 24th August 1964, shunter Ern Finney walking ahead to check that the road is clear before giving 'right away'; note the single headlamp.

By early in 1964 the panniers had left Weymouth altogether, their other duties being taken over by Ivatt 2P 2-6-2Ts, and, although the latter were given clearance to run over the tramway, the chance of steam reappearing seemed slender. However, a diesel failed and No. 41261 appeared on the quay, causing something of a stir. Between then (4th July) and September this engine and others of the class made several more trips. One reason was to save manpower. A diesel on the tramway needed two men but on yard shunting only one; a steam locomotive needed two anyway, so it saved a man to put steam on the tramway and keep the diesels in the yard. Although much heavier than the panniers, the 2Ps were well within tramway limits by virtue of their five axles. They were, of course, not really suitable for the job but their brief interlude as tram engines will long be remembered. The last one recorded in ordinary service was No. 41310, on 5th September 1964, but No. 41298 worked a special to the quay on 3rd July 1966 — almost certainly the last appearance of any steam locomotive on the tramway.

Of the standard Great Western engines the ones the men liked best were probably the 1366s. The big panniers would 'pull anything' but suffered from restricted visibility from the cab (less marked in the 8750s than in the earlier engines) while the 1361s were simply 'not strong enough'. The later steam locomotives are listed in Table II.

Consequent on the Bournemouth electrification, Weymouth shed closed completely as from midnight on 9th July 1967. Thereafter the Weymouth diesel shunters were nominally Bournemouth engines. For the tramway, and for general yard shunting, four or five of the Bournemouth allocation were to be found at Weymouth at any one time, one returning to Bournemouth each night for refuelling.

Table II
Weymouth Tramway Engines 1935-1964 (Steam)
(*see also Table I*)

1366 Class 0-6-0PT	*Weight:* (1) 35t 15c (2) 13t 0c (3) 3.25t		
	Tramway Service		
1366	Jun. – Oct. 1948, Nov. – Dec. 1954		
1367	Apr. 1935 – Mar. 1953, Sep. 1953 – Jun. 1962		
1368	Mar. 1947 – Mar. 1953, Dec. 1954 – Apr. 1962		
1369	Mar. 1960 – Jun. 1962		
1370	Jun. 1946 – Mar. 1953, Sep. 1953 – Dec. 1959		
1371	Apr. 1939 – Mar. 1947		
7400 Class 0-6-0PT	*Weight:* (1) 45t 9c (2) 15t 7c (3) 3.10t		
	*Tramway Service**		
7408	Mar. 1953 – Jan. 1955		
7415	Mar. – Sep. 1953		
7418	Mar. – Sep. 1953		
7421	Mar. 1953 – Jun. 1954		
5700 Class 0-6-0PT	*Weight:* (1) 47t 10c (2) 16t 15c (3) 3.07t		
	*Tramway Service***		*Tramway Service***
5781	1956	7780	1956-63
5784	1956-59	7782	1956-63
8750 Class 0-6-0PT	*Weight:* (1) 49t 0c (2) 16t 15c (3) 3.16t		
	*Tramway Service***		*Tramway Service***
3737	1962-63	4689	1960-63
3759	1961	8799	1960-62
4610	1963	9620	1960-63
4624	1960-63	9756	1960-62
4672	1960	possibly others, not recorded	
Class 2P 2-6-2T	*Weight:* (1) 63t 5c (2) 13t 5c (3) 2.09t		
			*Tramway Service***
41261/93/95/98, 41310			1964

Weight: (1) total (2) maximum axle (3) per foot run
* occasional use before 1953
** intermittent service; engines not allocated specifically for tramway

Plate 110: No. 15231 at the George Corner on 10th July 1967; note the three-link coupling.

Plate 111: A 350hp diesel-electric shunter, No. 15233, approaching the Town Bridge with the 'up' boat train, on 13th October 1967.

A second consequence of the electrification was the introduction of air-braked stock on the boat trains. In anticipation of this change, the 204hp engines being vacuum-fitted, four air-braked 350hp diesel-electrics were sent to Weymouth for the tramway. The first to arrive was No. 15230, on 25th June 1967; the others were Nos. 15231-3. These engines had their own problem, however. With the withdrawal of the winter boat trains it had become the practice to convey boat passengers by the late evening Bournemouth train, a portion of which was extended to Weymouth on sailing nights and worked through to the quay. After the electrification, the Weymouth Quay portion consisted of a 4-TC set (or two such sets) with waist level brake hoses. Since the engines' hoses were at buffer beam level an additional length of hose had to be interposed. A further small problem with No. 15231 was that it was not fitted with screw couplings.

The following summer the 204hp engines started to

Plate 112: The boat train formed of 4-TC units (Class 491) on 19th June 1970. Although it was normal practice for this stock to work through to the quay for night sailings during the winter, following the Bournemouth electrification, it was, until recently, not used at other times except when normal working was disrupted for some reason — e.g., industrial action. On this occasion the normal boat train had been cancelled because of 'trouble' at Waterloo. Note the small bell on the back of the cab.

Plate 113: No. D2397 with Class 491 stock at Westham crossing on 19th June 1970, showing the use of waist-level brake hoses; note also the air reservoir, one of which was fitted either side of the engine casing on dual-braked engines.

Plate 114: Dual-braked Class 3 No. D2399 on Custom House Quay with a rake of loaded Conflats on 19th March 1969.

appear with both brake systems, the air brake connections being duplicated (buffer beam as well as waist level). By July 1969 the nine then at Bournemouth were all dual-fitted, as shown in Table III. One thing they still could not provide, of course, was carriage heating. After the boiler van episode, steps were taken to install a static heating system at the pier. This was not ready until 1971, however, by which time it was no longer needed, it being only rarely that carriages stood at the pier in winter. As a result it was used only once or twice before mainline diesels took over the tramway (*see page 99*) and made it redundant.

On a basis of tractive effort the 204hp engines approximated closely to the 1366s but with a weight of around 31 tons were appreciably lighter. Both the Drewry and BR versions (Classes 4 and 3 respectively under the 1968 classification scheme) were always referred to indiscriminately as 'Drewries'. At 49 tons the diesel-electrics (Class 12) equated with the 8750s.

Apart from the occasional relief engine which was not vacuum-fitted — e.g., No. 679 — the tram engines, both steam and diesel, worked all traffic as required, no distinction being made between goods and passenger. Some may still be seen. Diesel Classes 4 and 12 are extinct, but

Plate 115: Trunnion-mounted bell as used on Nos. 1376 and 1377.

Author's Collection

Plate 116: The bell as mounted on pannier tanks.
C.L. Caddy

among the handful of Class 3s still in BR service (March 1986) are four that once 'worked the tram'. Also there is one survival from the days of steam. No. 1369 is preserved, on the Dart Valley Railway — and thus set to outlast the rest.

Perhaps the most familiar feature of the tram engines was the brass bell which, following the introduction of passenger trains, each of them was required to carry and which the fireman was required to ring all the time the engine was moving on the tramway. The bell was mounted on the engine in a variety of ways. In the earliest method recorded, it was mounted on trunnions which pivoted in a pair of cast-iron supports, a half-wheel at one side, rotated by a cord from the cab, causing the bell to rock to and fro. This rather elaborate mounting was used on the Bristol & Exeter tanks, *Fox*, *Hook Norton* and, as late as the 1930s, No. 1331. Later photographs of *Hook Norton*, during its second spell at Weymouth, show a simple bracket. A bracket was also used on Nos. 1386 and 679. On *Kidwelly* and *Cwm Mawr* the bracket was doubled to become a sort of stirrup, supporting the bell from opposite sides, but there was still a lack of uniformity. The mounting on *Kidwelly* was set 'fore and aft' while on *Cwm Mawr* it was set transversely. Although there is photographic evidence that for a time *Cwm Mawr* had only a simple bracket the difference is, in general, a useful aid to identification.

The position of the bell was as varied as the ways in which it was mounted. On the Bristol & Exeter tanks it was on top of the left-hand (fireman's side) tank; *Hook Norton* and No. 1386 had it at the front of the cab; and on *Fox* and Nos. 679 and 1331 it was on top of the tank, more or less centrally. On *Kidwelly* and *Cwm Mawr* and all later engines except the 2Ps, it was fitted underneath the left-hand tank, suspended from a simple bracket bolted to one of the tank supports, in the case of the panniers, and under the left-hand side of the tank, on the running plate, in the case of the saddle tanks. In one instance noted, an emergency bracket was improvised from a broken ring spanner. On the 2Ps a bracket or stirrup on top of the firebox was the only possible position. The Class 12 diesels and some of the Class 3s carried a very small bell on a brass bracket projecting from the back of the cab. Other Class 3s had the bell — sometimes small, sometimes large — in a stirrup on top of the engine casing in front of the cab or on a bracket fixed to the cab front. With the various types of fixed mounting the cord — usually just a piece of string — was attached to the bell clapper.

For an engine to appear on the quay minus bell, though not unknown, was rare, but by about the fifties, as road traffic became busier and noisier and pedestrians increasingly inured, the bell's usefulness was open to question. In October 1967, at the suggestion of the borough engineer's department, No. D2295 was fitted experimentally with an electric bell and, more relevant to modern traffic conditions, an amber flashing beacon. The experimental arrangement, involving two separate units, did not go into service and the idea appeared to have been dropped, more than three and a half years elapsing before another engine, this time No. D2180, appeared on the quay with a bell and beacon combined into a single unit (May 1971). After one or two minor modifications, these units were adopted generally. They were fitted to the centre lamp bracket and plugged into the engine's lighting system.

Plate 117: In the case of No. 3759 the layout of the pipework in connection with the left-hand injector precluded fitting the bell in its usual position, hence the position shown. This engine, photographed at the quay on 13th August 1961, was also unusual in having both Southern (rear socket) and Western (side socket) lamp irons — a total, including the additional Southern positions on the smokebox door, of twelve.

Plate 118: Experimental fitting of separate bell and flasher units on No. D2295, pictured on 17th October 1967.

Plate 119: Combined bell and flasher, developed from the experimental arrangement and used on the Class 3 shunters, photographed on No. D2399 on 28th May 1971.

Table III
Diesel locomotives on the tramway, 1962-1974

No.	*Built*	*Tramway Service*	*Dual Braking*
204hp diesel-mechanical			
D2043	Swindon, 1959	May 1966 – Jul. 1967	—
D2082	Doncaster, 1959	Apr. 1963 – Jul. 1967	—
D2280	Drewry Car Co. 1960	Dec. 1964 – May 1966	—
D2292	Drewry Car Co. 1960	Feb. – Jun. 1962	—
D2295	Drewry Car Co. 1960	Apr. 1962 – Mar. 1969*	—
D2397	Doncaster, 1961	May 1962 – Oct. 1972*	by Apr. 1969
D2398	Doncaster, 1961	May 1962 – Oct. 1971*	Oct. 1968
D2399	Doncaster, 1961	May 1962 – Apr. 1963	by Jun. 1968
		Mar. 1968 – Oct. 1972**	
* outstationed from Bournemouth after July 1967			
**outstationed from Bournemouth			
Bournemouth engines outstationed after July 1967, additional to Nos. D2295 and D2397-9, above (service between dates shown not continuous; some engines occasional only)			
D2028	Swindon, 1958	Jul. 1967 – Mar. 1969	—
D2084	Doncaster, 1959	May – Dec. 1969	by Jul. 1969
		Sep. 1971 – May 1973	
D2086	Swindon, 1959	Jun. 1968 – May 1973	Dec. 1968
		Apr. 1974*	
D2179	Swindon, 1962	Mar. 1969 – May 1973	by Mar. 1969
D2180	Swindon, 1962	Jul. 1967 – May 1973	Aug. 1968
D2196	Swindon, 1961	Jun. 1968 – Jun. 1973	Nov. 1968
D2197	Swindon, 1961	Feb. – Oct. 1968	by Mar. 1969
		Mar. 1969 – May 1973	
D2239	Drewry Car Co. 1956	Jul. 1967 – Apr. 1968	—
*as No. 03086			
350hp diesel-electric (outstationed from Bournemouth)			
15230	Ashford, 1951	Jun. 1967 – Jun. 1968	—
15231	Ashford, 1951	Jul. 1967 – Feb. 1968	—
15232	Ashford, 1951	Aug. 1967 – Oct. 1968	—
15233	Ashford, 1951	Aug. 1967 – Oct. 1968	—

From time to time there were isolated appearances of other Class 3s.

Another characteristic tramway fitting was a special footstep for the shunters, at the front, on the right-hand side. The earliest working instructions permitted the man who accompanied the engine to ride — when it was appropriate to do so — 'on the buffer plank', and the step was an extension of that practice. The early pattern was simply a length of bar iron bent round to form a flat 'hook'. This survived until the twenties, when steps of the more usual plate construction were substituted. Most of these were more or less narrow but Nos. 1376 and 1377 received very substantial steps about 2ft. across, supported on a heavy flared backplate. After the departure of these two engines one of the wide steps found its way onto No. 1331.

Associated with the steps were various kinds of hand-hold. The earliest form was a wooden post, about 15in. long and squared at one end to fit into the then standard lamp

Plate 120 (Left): 'Hook' shunter's step and post hand-hold as fitted to Nos. 1376 and 1377. The post in this case is held in position by a wooden wedge and length of rope.
Author's Collection

Plates 121 (Left) & 122 (Above): Nos. 1376 and 1377 on shed on Sunday, 18th April 1926. These views are included to show the later type of step fitted to these engines and No. 1331. The head-on view also shows the rail hand-hold very clearly. The gentleman in the bowler is Mr Harry Donne, the then shed foreman.
P.J.T. Reed

Plate 123: The boat train drawing away from the pier in 1921, behind *Hook Norton*. This engine retained the primitive 'hook' step throughout and as regards hand-hold it appears to have been a case of 'hang on where you can'.

R. Brookman

Plate 124: The BP&GV engines were fitted at first with 'hook' steps, as in this view of *Kidwelly* on shed on 18th April 1926, soon after arriving at Weymouth.

P.J.T. Reed

Plate 125: The later type of step fitted to these engines is shown in this view of *Cwm Mawr* at the pier on 9th July 1935. Note also the spare three-link couplings on the running plate.

Author's Collection

Plate 126: Shunters 'Spike' Milligan and Alf Ayling riding the front steps of No. 41298, on 24th August 1964.

socket. From about 1904 new engines were fitted with lamp irons instead of sockets but some years elapsed before all existing engines were changed. *Hook Norton*, the Bristol & Exeter tanks and No. 1386 were still fitted with sockets until about 1909, possibly later. The post was replaced by an iron rail, either curved or bent round at 90 degrees, between the running plate and the smokebox front. The 1366s were fitted with the standard horizontal bar, on the running plate.

Among the early engines the only one not fitted with a step and hand-hold appears to have been *Fox* — with the buffer beam hard against the cylinder head there simply wasn't room — but not all the 1366s received them. Conversely, although No. 1361 was on the tramway for only three months, in 1960, considerable trouble was taken to see that it was properly equipped, even to the extent of appropriating a bar hand-hold from 2-6-2T No. 4507. The large panniers, not being specifically tramway engines, did not receive the front step, the shunters usually riding on the cab steps or, as was not uncommon even on engines with a step, half inside the cab itself. On the 2Ps a front step was standard, as were, of course, the special recessed steps on the diesels.

One other essential requirement for the tram engines was steam heating, though again there were exceptions, notably, in recent years, No. 1369, which was without it until February 1962, when it returned from repair at Wolverhampton.

When cleanliness was a virtue the tram engines were always given special attention, as they were very much on public view, and for the connoisseur their interest was enhanced by the assortment of 'bits and pieces' usually strewn about them — shunter's pole (or poles), spare lamps, a tramway coupling or two, loose point levers and the tow-rope, in addition to the usual fire irons and bucket. The tow-rope was a steel cable about 24ft. long, fitted at one end with a link for attachment to the engine drawhook and at the other with a hook for insertion in the wagon solebar, enabling an engine on one track to move wagons on the adjacent one. It is not known when it was first used at Weymouth but it may be seen draped along the running plate and hooked over a lamp iron or the smokebox door handles in any photograph taken after about 1900. As congestion increased, and movement became more restricted, this method of shunting was increasingly resorted to. The 1933 improvements reduced the need for it but it was not finally discarded until 1952, after the rebuilding of Custom House Quay. Until then the prohibition of Templeman's siding to locomotives meant that movement of wagons over it usually required the rope. Up to forty-five wagons were sometimes moved in this way. The practice was, of course, not peculiar to Weymouth Quay but elsewhere was confined to stations of comparative unimportance.

For many years all trains and light engines running over the tramway were required to display 'the usual head and tail signals' (which, on passenger trains, included side lamps). For passenger trains 'usual' was interpreted as Class B headcode, and for goods a single lamp somewhere along the buffer beam, but the distinction was not taken too seriously. In the 1947 instructions the requirement became simply 'head and tail lamps must be used . . .' Class B was still generally applied to passenger trains, but very often one of the lower — and more easily accessible — positions was used instead; in fact, regardless of the type of traffic, trains could be seen on occasion carrying anything from Class A to nothing at all. Until the introduction of the flashing beacon the diesels usually displayed two 'side lights', motor car fashion, very often with one or more oil lamps superimposed.

Plate 127: A Weymouth Quay lamp in use as a tail lamp, hanging from the drawhook, on 7th April 1961.

Plate 129: The DANGER board for loose-coupled goods trains, seen on 27th July 1961; note the Weymouth Quay lamp attached to the lamp iron, using the protective guards as a socket. This was the first type of board to go into service, after one or two experiments with different methods of attachment, such as a rigid bar with curved ends to drop over the buffer shanks.

Plate 128: A Weymouth Quay lamp as more often seen, as a spare on the engine running plate, on 20th June 1960.

Plate 130: The board as not intended to be used but as often seen — adorning the smokebox door, on 12th August 1961.

Allied to the question of head lamps was the introduction, in 1960, of a special Weymouth Quay tail lamp. Trouble had been experienced with vehicles following too closely behind loose-coupled trains and not allowing for buffer rebound when the train stopped. The lamps were designed to be used on conjunction with a red board reading CAUTION KEEP 50FT. CLEAR and were fitted with an elongated handle so that when hung from the drawhook they would show below the board. That, at least, was the theory. The boards did not appear until over a year later (July 1961) and when they did were invariably used alone. A later pattern was itself hung from the drawhook. To protect the bull's-eyes from contact with the coupling, the lamp casing was provided with a pair of rectangular iron guards. Not being intended to be placed on a lamp iron the lamps had no socket; no matter — they could always be attached to an iron using the protective guards instead, with the iron between the guards and the 'protected' glass. One bull's-eye was white but in practice the lamps were not used as head lamps. They were, in fact, not used to any great extent even as tail lamps and were more often to be seen among the spare lamps on the engine running plate. By the end of 1964 they were more or less in disuse. The boards survived until the end of freight working though by then, battered and shabby, they were often not carried.

WEYMOUTH JUNCTION

Plate 131 (Above): The 'down' boat train standing on the main line at the inner home on 11th June 1959. The engine, No. 5084, *Reading Abbey*, is drawing forward with the dining cars, signalled into the goods yard, while the rest of the train awaits the tram engine for its journey to the quay.
S. Rickard

Plate 132 (Right): In February 1956, the instructions were amended to permit the use of the loops inside the yard gates for engine changing, and thereafter the change was often made there, particularly on Saturdays. The tram engines and bankers also used Melcombe siding (*see Plan A on page 52*). In this view, on 9th August 1958, No. 5093, *Upton Castle*, is drawing forward into the inner loop with the dining cars while No. 1368 waits in Melcombe siding to take over.

Plate 133: A similar view in Southern days, on 28th July 1962 — No. 34010, *Sidmouth*, has drawn forward on to the coal road, leaving the train to be taken forward by No. 3737.

Plate 134: One of the first appearances of a 'Crompton' on the boat train, Sunday, 10th July 1966 (No. D6521, later 33108). The tram engine is No. D2082.

Plate 135: Saturday, 15th July 1961 produced an interesting variation. The inward boat due at 5a.m. was delayed by heavy weather, and did not arrive until midday. As three 'down' boat trains were due at the quay between 11.36a.m. and 12.10p.m., requiring all three platforms, the 'up' train, which should have left at 5.55a.m., was taken to the closed Melcombe Regis Station, on the Portland branch, passengers being conveyed there from the quay by bus. The train is here seen starting for Waterloo from the branch behind No. 30852, *Sir Walter Raleigh*.

Plate 136: The engines for the Paddington boat train stand on the engine road, on 11th September 1956, having just come off shed and before crossing over to await the train's arrival from the quay. The train engine is No. 5082 *Swordfish*, and the banker is No. 5314, one of the 'regulars'.

Plate 137: The 'up' 'Channel Islands Boat Express' bound for Paddington for the last time, on 26th September 1959. The engine is No. 7010 *Avondale Castle*.

Plate 138: Sharing the tramway working with No. 3737 on 28th July 1962 (*see Plate 133*) was diesel shunter No. D2397. The two engines are seen standing together in Melcombe siding while awaiting the arrival of their trains from Waterloo.

Plate 139: For a brief period before the 'up' winter boat train was discontinued (*see page 52*) it consisted of only three carriages and a van, which, however, unlike the Paddington train (*see Plate 88*), ran through to London. The 'short' train was photographed on its arrival at the junction behind No. 4689, on 31st October 1962.

Plate 140: The 'Channel Islands Boat Express' moves off from the 'up' loop starting signal, on 4th July 1964, as the late Joe Frier, yard inspector, disputes a point with the driver of *Royal Observer Corps*.

Plate 141: The 'up' train awaiting 'right away' for the main line on 28th October 1965 (passed back to the banker by a crow from the train engine). The banker, No. 76005, has been waiting in Melcombe siding and has just come on to the rear of the train for the 1 in 50 climb to Bincombe Tunnel. In the left foreground is the Portland branch. Other classes used to bank the boat trains included, at different times, 'Bulldogs', Churchward Moguls (a long-standing favourite), 41XX, 'Q', 'Merchant Navy', 'West Country', 2P 2-6-2T and Standard 4-6-0s of Classes 4 and 5.

Plate 142: On Saturday, 8th July 1967 No. 35023, having worked the last steam-hauled train from Waterloo, returned with the boat train — another 'last steam'. No. 35023 is here seen moving off from the 'up' branch starting signal.

CHAPTER ELEVEN

The Tramway Today

With the end of general freight the tramway was, as already remarked, to a large extent redundant, and from then on it became virtually a 'summer only' operation. For a time, in the early seventies, even the practice of extending to the quay on winter sailing nights was discontinued except in respect of one or two specified sailings — e.g., the Christmas peak. From the winter of 1973-74 until night sailings came to an end (*page 103*) there was a more or less general return to that practice, although, when passengers were few, the advertised train was liable to be replaced by a bus hired from Southern National. In the opposite direction a bus to the town station, with a Waterloo connection at around 15.35, was already — and has remained — the winter norm (but *see page 109*).

Since 1972, at intervals, nearly all unwanted track has been removed, reducing the tramway to little more than the length of plain line that it was when first opened. The first such removal was, in fact, already in hand when freight traffic was withdrawn. This was of the two sidings laid alongside the Backwater in 1962, which were lifted in February 1972. In retrospect it may be doubted whether their construction was justified. Initially, with the concentration of the whole of the Guernsey tomato traffic on Weymouth, they were useful for standing empty vans. It was not foreseeable that that requirement would not last, and a potential second use — the standing of loaded vans pending shipment — was frowned on by the Transport Police on security grounds. By about the mid-sixties, as traffic declined generally, they had fallen into disuse. The turn-outs at the quay end remained until relaying of that length in October 1984; those at the station end are in position still (June 1986) — a mute reminder of promise unfulfilled.

The next contraction took place at the pier. Shortly before the closure of the cargo service, British Rail had begun negotiations with the corporation for the construction of a roll-on/roll-off terminal for a new ferry service to Jersey. These were pursued to a successful conclusion, and work started in November 1972. Essentially the requirement was for reclamation of further space from Weymouth Bay but inclusion of part of the existing quay meant curtailment of the tramway. On 24th November contractors began lifting and within days around 185ft. of double track at the end of the pier, including the fancy diamond crossing, had been cut up for scrap. No. 3 road was cut back by a further 430ft. or so, to a dead end, and equipped with a new fuel-oil pipeline installation for the steamers, together with the necessary pumping and reserve storage.

Ever since the introduction of oil-burning vessels, in 1925, oil had been brought to Weymouth by ordinary freight trains, the loaded tank wagons then standing in the yard as a 'pool' to be drawn on as required. After the closure of Weymouth goods station, in July 1971, the retention of such through-load freight as remained was closely allied to the

Plate 143: On 5th March 1972, five days after the end of freight traffic, the Backwater sidings have already been lifted, and all that remains is to load away the redundant sleepers. The engine is No. 2179.

C.L. Caddy

Plates 144 & 145: After the lifting of the tramway loop sidings, (*see page 95*) the stub of the former Portland branch was connected into the tramway with a view to extending the 'up' and 'down' loops and eliminating the scissors crossing. Completion of the realignment required the repositioning of the tramway 'up' home signal, standing in line with the left-hand rail. That was never done and by the time these photographs were taken, on 19th July 1983, the idea had long been abandoned and the track partly lifted. (i) Shows the car park level crossing, with the signal 'staying put' and (ii) The abandoned remains, viewed from the other side of the crossing. Half the scissors (background) remains, and continues to serve as a connection between the tramway (right) and the 'up' loop.

Plate 146 (Below): In February 1986, when a new access road was laid in association with the redevelopment of former railway land (the site of the goods station and part of the old passenger station) the overflow car park was closed and the sleeper crossing superseded by a new one in prefabricated concrete (Bomac), paid for by the developer. The first train to use the new crossing was an excursion by the Venice Simplon-Orient-Express, promoted jointly by Thomas Cook and Two Counties Radio, on 26th April 1986.

Plate 147: STOP signs, one 'up' and one 'down', prevail over a clear signal until the shunters accompanying the train have halted traffic on the crossing. The 'up' sign is shown here in its original position, before the installation of the Bomac crossing. It has now been repositioned.

Plate 148: The 'down' boat train on 19th July 1983, with the unofficial headboard, first used, on No. 33117, on 24th May 1982. The product of commendable 'private enterprise' by one of the staff at Bournemouth, the board was attached there to the engine of the 'down' train, after engines had been changed, and removed there on the 'up' working. It remained in use until the end of the 1985 season, when the regular hauled train ran for the last time.

Plate 149: This aged Great Western wagon, fitted with a Tangye Duplex steam pump, spent around thirty eight years trundling up and down the tramway sandwiched between oil tank wagons. The pump was driven by steam drawn from the ship into which the oil was being pumped. It is pictured on 17th May 1958.

Plate 150: (Above): In May 1963 the old wagon was condemned and the pump transferred to a newer one, but within months, completely worn out, it was scrapped. The replacement wagon is seen on 28th February 1964.

Plate 151: A replacement pump, diesel-driven and housed in a redundant box van, served until 1973, when the fixed installation was brought into use. The photograph, taken on 4th May 1964, shows the pump with hoses connected, pumping from tank wagon to ship.

Plate 152 (Below): Class 3 No. 2196 on the first oil train to use the new installation, then still incomplete, on 1st June 1973.

Plate 153: One of the regular oil trains, consisting of fourteen 40-ton glw tank wagons behind a Class 33 diesel locomotive — in this case No. 6516 — photographed in July 1973.

survival of the Channel Islands cargo service, and when that closed Weymouth goods quickly followed (14th August 1972). The old procedure thus came to an end, and utilising No. 3 road as an oil siding was an effective alternative. Discharge points into the system were spaced to accommodate block trains of fourteen standard 45-ton glw two-axle tank cars (under-loaded to 40 tons gross to conform to the maximum permitted axle loading of 20 tons). Reserve storage was improvised by standing four old tank wagons on a detached length of track beyond the stop blocks. The installation was brought into partial use on 1st June 1973 and full use on the 29th, deliveries in the interim having been made by road tanker.

Sidings inside the yard gates (*page 52 Plan A*), latterly used mainly for engine changing, were lifted early in 1974, when the former goods yard was laid out as a car park and fenced off. Two years later an additional car park was opened in part of the yard on the 'up' side, with access by a sleeper crossing over the tramway. Since then the crossing (or its modern replacement — *see Plate 146*) has been regarded, operationally, as the dividing line between the ordinary running road and the tramway.

A vestige of siding remained outside the yard gates, at the end of Commercial Road, until the road was resurfaced, in April 1978. Later that year, what was once Greenwood's siding also disappeared in the course of road resurfacing. The rest of the 'back road', between St. Alban Street and Ferry's Corner, remained as a dead-end siding, unused, until October 1984, when the remaining connection, at the pier end, was removed. Templeman's, hitherto intact, although not used since 1969, was at the same time disconnected at the station end. Thus, of the once numerous sidings and loops nothing is left but two disused dead-ends (Templeman's and the cargo stage — *see page 98*) and the abandoned remains of the back road.

TEMPLEMAN'S SIDING

Plate 154: No. 1367 standing at the blocks at the end of the siding on 28th March 1961 — a most unusual place for an engine to stand.

Plates 155-157: With the decline in Channel Islands freight traffic the siding tended to be less used for standing wagons, but until about 1969 it was used regularly — if infrequently — for various cargoes imported in non-railway vessels and forwarded by rail: (i) Timber from the Baltic; (ii) Beet pulp from Holland; (iii) Cider apples from France.

Plate 158: The siding in use as a through loop during relaying; No. D2397 on a train of loaded Conflats, on 12th February 1969. Note (left) rail lengths set up on blocks for Thermit welding of joints before laying on concrete foundations (right). (*See also Plate 40*).

Closure of Weymouth goods posed a problem as to future motive power for the tramway. Without yard shunting the Class 3s had little other work left, and it would be an economy to eliminate them altogether. Since the Bournemouth electrification, traffic between Bournemouth and Weymouth had been worked almost entirely by 'Cromptons' (BRCW 1,550hp Type 3, later Class 33). Cromptons had, in fact, first appeared on the boat trains, on Sundays, a year earlier, in July 1966. The obvious next step, if it proved to be practicable, was for them to work through to the quay instead of handing over at the junction to a Class 3.

Plate 159: No. 6533 on the test train. 'How was it?' — arrival at the pier was followed by the inevitable 'confab' before the train returned to the junction.

Plate 160: 'Each engine . . . is provided with a bell, which the fireman must ring continuously . . .' But what about a 'Crompton'? We'll just have to pretend. The bell on No. 6533 on the occasion of the trial.

On 15th February 1973, accompanied by an assemblage of British Rail personnel and to the clicking of cameras, No. 6533 and a 3-TC set emerged from the yard and proceeded down Commercial Road, on trial. Considerations at issue were weight, possible noise and vibration, and steady control at tramway speed. The trial was successful but, before the Class 33s could start regular working, track alterations were necessary to enable them to run round. The old engine release crossover having disappeared to make way for the ferry terminal the end of No. 2 road was connected into No. 1, to form a loop. The connection, an awkward one, on a curve, has been the scene of at least one derailment. More important, No. 1 road was now too short for twelve carriages — the then standard boat train formation — to stand inside the loop's clearance points. By 'spreading' the approach to Nos. 1 and 2 roads at the pier entrance, however, it was possible, again with recourse to some decidedly awkward alignment, to stretch the loop just enough to obtain the required clearance, with the last carriage standing off the platform until the engine had run round and set the train back to the blocks (*page 47 Plan B*). To enable the loop points to be repositioned those at the pier end of the stage road were removed, leaving the stage as a dead-end siding.

Plate 161: 'Spreading' the approach to Nos. 1 and 2 roads at the pier, on 24th January 1973, to give clearance for the engine to run round twelve-coach trains; left — the old alignment; right — the new alignment.

Plate 162: Not a prize-winning effort, but it serves. The re-alignment complete.

Plate 163 (Above): No. 6538 running round its twelve-coach train on 12th April 1973, amid the clutter of work on the still unfinished ferry terminal.

Plate 164 (Left): The plug-in bell/flasher unit, as used from 1973 to 1983, being attached to the 'station' end of No. 6529 by second man Gerald House, on 25th August 1973, after removal from the 'quay' end, and prior to the engine running round; shunter David James assisting.

On 12th April 1973 empty stock was worked to the quay by No. 6538 to test the new layout and the first of the class to run through in normal service was No. 6527, on 7th May (the first day of the summer timetable). For the next week or two, until all the engines concerned had been fitted for the flashing beacon, there were still intermittent appearances of Class 3s. One Class 3 continued to work at Weymouth for about another year, as station pilot etc., and the last recorded working of the class on the tramway was of No. 03086, on 10th April 1974, when the boat train engine was commandeered to replace a failed Class 33 on an up Waterloo working.

Since 1973, apart from that and one other isolated exception (*see Plates 184 & 185*), tramway motive power has been provided entirely by engines of Class 33, in the main by the nineteen Eastleigh-based engines of Class 33/1 (the Bournemouth – Weymouth push/pull engines). Engines of Class 33/0 have appeared on a number of occasions, and there has been one recorded appearance of Class 33/2 (Hastings gauge). No. 33204, temporarily available at Eastleigh after repair, worked the down and up boat trains on 16th July 1979. From time to time there have been excursion workings to the quay from other regions, usually hauled by a Class 47. On such occasions a Class 33 has taken over at the junction and become a tram engine — a far cry

Plate 165: The last recorded appearance of a Class 3 diesel shunter on the tramway — No. 03086 on the boat train on 10th April 1974.

Plate 166: No. 33102 heading the boat train down Commercial Road, with shunters Steve Hales and Michael Penney in attendance, on 21st June 1974.

Plate 167 (Above): No. 33115 acting as tram engine on a Cherbourg excursion, consisting of Western Region stock, which had arrived at the junction behind No. 47020.is shown here at Ferry's Corner, on 22nd April 1978.

Plate 168 (Below): Cameras to the fore as Class 101 diesel multiple unit No. C812 passes along Custom House Quay on trial, on 3rd March 1983. Note the handbell carried by the shunter. As far as is known all units used in regular service to the quay were Bristol-based but interestingly the trial was run by one from Cardiff.

from No. 2. Crews are normally changed for the tramway, although on some workings the main line driver is simply joined by a second man. The prescribed procedure is for the train to stop at the shunters' cabin, adjacent to the 'down' tramway starting signal, for attachment of the lantern, and then again at the level crossing for the lantern to be switched on; also for the heater jumper cables between the engine and the train to be disconnected for running over the tramway (a safety precaution). In practice, however, the procedure varies. Trains working via the town station change crews there, and even with the direct boat train 'the book' was not strictly followed. For instance, going down, crew changing, etc. invariably took place at the King Street crossing rather than the car park crossing (requiring a shorter walk from the station).

In 1983 the Waterloo boat train was joined by a through service from Bristol, with a connection from Cardiff. Reintroduction of such a service had long been under consideration, and on 3rd March Western Region 3-car DMU No. C812 was run to the quay and back to test clearances etc. The pier not having had to handle two passenger trains at once since the 1973 alterations, the unit was preceded by a 'boat train' made up of assorted vans (the inclusion of postal vans prompting all kinds of rumour!) as a further feasibility check. This was the first appearance of one of these units on the tramway, although Hastings units have been used for enthusiasts' specials. A regular service, by extension from the town station, which was served en route in both directions, ran during July and August.

The year also brought a surprise reappearance of freight

Plate 169 (Above): Class 117 diesel multiple unit No. B428 on Commercial Road, on 19th July 1983.

Plate 170 (Right): Class 117 diesel multiple unit No. B430 standing on No. 2 road at the pier, alongside No. 33118 with the Waterloo boat train, on 18th July 1983. As will be seen, (*compare Plate 165*) the boat train no longer occupies the whole platform, or requires the 1973 realignment for running round, having been reduced first to ten and then, in 1979, to eight, plus buffet car. A buffet car was included only until 1982, when Sealink withdrew the subsidy on which it had latterly depended.

Plate 171: The usual diesel multiple unit working consisted of a single 3-car set but sometimes, on a Sunday, three sets worked through to save dividing the train at the town station. A 9-car train, headed by Class 119 unit No. B577, is here seen standing at No. 2 platform on 2nd September 1984. Note the flasher unit.

Plate 172: (Below): Bristol and South Wales, No. 2 Platform — train information at the quay on 16th July 1983.

— a block consignment of export cars. On 8th March 105 BL 'Minis' and 'Metros' were conveyed to Weymouth on twenty-one Carflats, the train being split at the junction to keep within the reduced berthing space at the pier. Carflats had appeared on the tramway before, in the days of the ordinary freight service, and with unloading by crane, but a complete train, with drive-off unloading, was an innovation offering the prospect of future expansion. With the car ferry terminal abutting on the blocks at the end of No. 1 road, the operation could not have been simpler, unloading requiring nothing more than a makeshift ramp and the temporary removal of the intervening chain-link fence. Its success resulted in the exporter deciding to send further consignments by rail, to which end the fence was later provided with a proper gateway, but because of obstruction by the road transport union there has to date been only one further consignment, and that, by sheer mischance, was while the end of the tramway was temporarily blocked (*see page 104*).

Against these two 'firsts' in 1983 has to be set one 'last' — the last of the oil trains. Like the boat trains these were a summer-only operation, the smaller quantities required in winter being more economically delivered by road. In 1973, when they started, the Weymouth ships were all steam turbine. As the steamers were successively replaced by motor vessels, consumption of fuel oil fell, and the trains, originally twice weekly, became less frequent. With the departure of the last turbine vessel, at the end of the 1981 season, it was only a matter of time for road to take over altogether. The last railborne oil was received at the quay on 16th September 1983.

Further 'lasts' were to follow. During the summer of 1984 a second DMU ran through, in connection with the night sailings. In the up direction this formed the 07.00 departure from the town station but its frequent lateness from the quay alienated many town and other up-line passengers. With hindsight this particular Bristol connection must be seen as misguided, and its first season proved to be also its last. Whether the daytime DMU connection would have continued beyond 1984 must be a matter for speculation as, in the event, outside factors intervened. Following the privatisation of Sealink, in July 1984, it was decided to discontinue night sailings and concentrate Channel Islands arrivals and departures into a short period around midday.

Plate 173: Export cars being driven off 'Motorail' flats over the makeshift ramp, on 8th March 1983.

Plate 174: This consignment of 193 export cars, on 22nd February 1985, could not be off-loaded at the quay because of the temporary closure of the quay station. Instead, a ramp of scaffolding and planks was built on the tramway adjacent to the car park level crossing (*see Plate 144*), enabling the cars to be driven off into the car park.

Other considerations apart, this made a daytime Bristol connection impracticable. With the end of night sailings the winter Bristol connection also disappeared. Latterly, both Waterloo and Bristol were shown as having a quay connection on Friday and Sunday nights, though in practice only one ran through (usually the Bristol) and sometimes neither. Sailings continued until the end of March 1985 but the train connection was ended prematurely, by temporary closure of the quay station for structural repairs. The last was the 20.30 from Bristol on Sunday 16th December 1984, consisting of No. 33002 with 'six on' and from the town to the quay carrying just fourteen passengers.

Although they ran for only two seasons the DMUs were at least partly behind a notable change in tramway practice — the discontinuance of the warning bell. The bell/flasher units used on the Class 33/1s, being designed to be clamped to the central buffer and plugged into a special socket, could not be used on any other vehicle. A redesigned unit, battery-operated and with a socket to fit the lamp iron, was accordingly put in hand for 1984. In the meantime the existing units mysteriously disappeared. The last use officially recorded was on 31st August, after which they were 'no longer available', but their abrupt end remains unexplained. In such a contingency, or when accompanying a train to which the unit could not be attached, the shunters were required to carry a handbell instead. This they strongly objected to. Having to walk through the streets 'like a muffin man' was, understandably, embarrassing, and they had in any case come to regard the bell as ineffectual in today's conditions. After much deliberation their view prevailed, and it was decided that the new units should consist of a flashing beacon only. These were used for the first time on 7th April 1984.

Their introduction opened the way for TC stock of Class 491 to be propelled over the tramway, thus eliminating running round when that stock is used. The initial trial of Class 33, in 1973, involved propelling the train back to the junction as the remaining crossover at the pier was

Plate 175 (Left): The new-style flasher unit, without bell, attached to No. 33101, on 14th April 1984.

Plate 176 (Below): 4-TC set No. 424, being propelled by No. 33116 and carrying the new-style flasher unit, at King Street crossing, on 30th April 1984.

Plate 177 (Above): The trial unit leaving the 'up' loop on its return to Bournemouth.

Plate 178 (Right): During the first three weeks of the 1985 season, before the regular boat train was running, the quay was served entirely by Class 491 stock, with bewildering variations in the working pattern. This view, taken on 9th May 1985, shows two such trains, each of two 4-TC sets, standing at the pier together. Variations included 'engine up' (instead of 'engine down', as here) and the use of one set per train instead of two.

temporarily obstructed by work on the ferry terminal, but in ordinary service, as long as the plug-in units were in use, the engine was required to lead in both directions. On 30th April 1984 No. 33116 ran from Bournemouth to the quay and back with a 4-TC set, propelling both ways. The main purpose of the trial was to assess tramway visibility from the trailer's driving compartment. Despite misgivings on the part of a few drivers, the trial was deemed a success and with this class of stock propelling is now established tramway practice (though there are some who, when the 'quiet' end is leading, regret the passing of the bell).

The cost of operating and maintaining the tramway falls on Southern Region. Following the transfer of British Rail ships to separate management, in 1969, (Shipping & International Services Division, later Sealink U.K. Ltd) a fare differential was introduced as between the quay and the town station — in effect, a tramway toll. Currently standing at 60p for the single journey this is credited to Southern Region as part of the rail element in through fares irrespective of whether conveyance to or from the quay is by the tramway or substitute bus service. A 60p single fare is also available between the two stations. This is intended to facilitate the payment of excess by passengers not booked through, but as long as trains serve both stations it provides incidentally an opportunity to travel the tramway independently.

The maintenance liability includes the road surface for 2ft. 6in. on either side of the track but in practice, except

Plates 179 & 180: Conflict with other road users: (i) A pantechnicon parked too close for comfort, resulting in a nasty scraping noise — an incident near the Town Bridge, on 29th July 1965. (ii) An offending vehicle about to be removed by recovery vehicle, on 2nd July 1983. The train is rounding the 1939 curve.

(i) Author
(ii) Dorset Evening Echo

when relaying is involved, it is usually more convenient for the work to be done by the corporation, with Southern Region contributing to the cost. As regards operation, a peculiar addition to normal costs is policing. What may be called 'conflict with other road users' has been a problem, in one form or another, since the line first opened, but in the last twenty-five years or so the never-ending growth of ordinary road traffic has greatly intensified it. In summer, obstruction by badly parked vehicles can cause serious delay. Formerly their removal was a matter for the local police, who tended to regard the trains as an irrelevance and were reluctant to get involved. They were at the same time unwilling to allow the Transport Police to act instead and on occasion, inevitably, there was friction. Absurd as it may seem, the point was reached when there was even talk of prosecuting the Transport Commission for *causing* obstruction. For the Transport Police to have specific responsibility *for the trains*, and, where appropriate, to prosecute offenders, was a common-sense compromise, and since May 1963 that has been the position. Since then officers of the Transport Police have gone ahead of the boat train to try to ensure an unimpeded run, formerly cycling but since 1974 by car, with blue light flashing and head lamps on. For a time (1976-77) the car also carried a roof board, warning CAUTION BOAT TRAIN, but the public were not noticeably influenced by it and the idea was dropped. Recently, however (September 1985), it has been resurrected, in the form of a smaller and less elaborate board.

Plate 181: The 'up' boat train on Custom House Quay, on 9th August 1977, preceded by the Transport Police car carrying the CAUTION board Note the yellow hatching across the track.

Plate 182: Summer on the tramway — a picture that says it all. A Bristol diesel multiple unit, No. B439, at Westham crossing on 16th August 1983.

Having regard to the peculiar circumstances, parking foul of the track is dealt with not under any of the normal 'railway obstruction' provisions — e.g., the 1840 Railway Regulation Act — but under the appropriate road traffic legislation relating to causing unnecessary obstruction by a motor vehicle. Offenders can expect a fine of £25 in addition to the cost of removal by the recovery vehicle. Removal inevitably takes time, and delays of an hour or more, though unusual, are not unknown. A car can sometimes be 'bumped' aside (if the shunters are willing to do this the public can invariably be relied on to lend a hand) but at least one other potential remedy, a trolley jack carried in the police car, has been found to be impracticable.

In today's conditions two once-separate problems, obstruction *of* the tramway and obstruction *by* the tramway, are compounded, for if the train is halted it becomes itself a serious obstruction. Prevention, if it were possible, would therefore serve everybody's interest. Yellow hatching across the track has proved to be of limited value, since it lacks statutory force; also, its periodic renewal is expensive. In 1985, somewhat belatedly, a more positive approach to the problem, by Sealink and the corporation together, resulted in the wider use of statutory double yellow lines and the appearance of additional warning notices. These have effected some improvement, but as long as there are car drivers to whom the message NO PARKING is unintelligible — or invisible — the problem will remain.

Given the evident difficulty and expense of operating the tramway today the question may be asked why it is retained — indeed, its future was in question, after a critical appraisal of costs, as far back as 1971. The answer is that it is still seen as making a useful contribution to the service. For Sealink the convenience of cross-platform passenger transfer speaks for itself. Less obviously, that facility also benefits Southern Region, for without it many Channel Islands passengers might desert rail altogether; also, it seems, it is cheaper and more convenient to run a summer boat train than to accommodate extra passengers on the ordinary Weymouth service and transfer them by bus. In this connection it is interesting to note that in the current British Rail time table (May 1986) Table 158 (London to Weymouth) includes Channel Islands sailing and arrival times as an integrated item, instead of merely referring to relevant trains by a footnote, as hitherto. Many, among them local councillors, see the tramway as having 'tourist interest', a view supported by its depiction on more than one seaside postcard (although others, inevitably, regard the trains as an unmitigated nuisance). Perhaps more significantly, what has long been endured as a 'vexatious and uncomfortable crawl' (*page 52*) is now featured in Sealink's Channel Islands brochure as one of the attractions of the Weymouth route — 'a memorable journey through the streets of the town'. And who's to say it is not?

Questions nevertheless remain. At the end of the 1985 season Sealink revealed that the Channel Islands services had incurred massive losses (mainly at Portsmouth) and that in 1986 Weymouth sailings would be reduced to once daily. The train service has been correspondingly reduced and, ironically, it is the hauled boat train that has disappeared, since the 'down and up' connection that it provided cannot be reconciled with the revised steamer times. Its last day of working was 15th September 1985. Only the TC service remains, by extension from the town station, involving time-wasting shunting movements and uneconomic empty stock working. A somewhat improved winter shipping service as compared with recent years does not, on the other hand, justify restoration of a winter connection (a Waterloo service scheduled for the winter of 1985/6 did not materialise, because the quay was once again closed for repairs), and use of the tramway is now at its lowest level ever.

Despite this, British Rail do not propose closure, at least for the time being, but will continue to run the trains 'as long as Sealink require them' and subject to 'continuous review'. How long that is likely to be must be anybody's guess, of course; the more immediate threat is posed from within. In January 1986 the Government announced its long-awaited approval of British Rail's proposal to electrify the line between Bournemouth and Weymouth. Electrification, expected to come into operation in January

Plate 183: Boat train extra-ordinary. On 24th May 1985, as part of the publicity attending the renaming of one of the ships, Channel Islands passengers from Waterloo were invited to sample the period comforts of the company's 'Venice Simplon-Orient-Express', here seen approaching Westham crossing behind No. 33029. From Bournemouth the engine carried the unofficial CHANNEL ISLANDS BOAT TRAIN headboard (*see Plate 148*), the Sealink banner being substituted at the junction.

Plates 184 & 185: The shape of things to come? On the evening of Friday, 15th June 1984, the engine of the 'down' boat train failed at Dorchester. The train was rescued by a spare Class 33 locomotive from Weymouth, which, however, being rostered for other duties, could not follow the usual practice of remaining at the quay overnight. To work the early 'up' train, following a spate of failures, Eastleigh provided a pair of Class 73 electro-diesels (Nos. 73125 and 73138), two being necessary because of the limited power when working diesel, although for the tramway one would have sufficed. The train is seen here (i) On Custom House Quay and (ii) On Commercial Road. If the tramway is to remain in use after the line to Weymouth is electrified, electro-diesels are one of the available options.

B.L. Jackson

1988, cannot be extended to the quay, for obvious reasons. The tramway can therefore remain in use only by continued dependence on diesel traction.

Various possibilities exist, but all would appear to require the availability of at least two locomotives, not only as a precaution against failure but because the current schedule — a concomitant of the one-ship service — involves the presence of two trains at the quay together and the occupation of both roads, which precludes running round. It has in any case yet to be decided whether the new electric stock can be worked to the quay. Other considerations apart, with a length of 23m. (75ft.) it will exceed the maximum currently permitted by some 8ft. If the present restriction cannot be lifted, C1 stock will have to be made available, in addition to diesel locomotives. The threat of 'bussing' therefore looms, even though past experience suggests that buses are unlikely to prove the instant trouble-free alternative that some suppose, and for Sealink the loss of cross-platform convenience could prove critical. Meanwhile (June 1986) speculation lends the subject topical interest, and with the line now closed for eight months in the year the return of the trains, like summer swallows or the first cuckoo, merits a mention in the local press:

> 'Trains trundled along Commercial Road yesterday as the tramway line between the town and quay stations came back into operation for the summer season . . .'

began a recent item, complete with picture, in the *Dorset Evening Echo*.

Contemplation of the tramway's precarious future prompts a concluding reflection on its importance in the past. How much of all the rail traffic into and out of Weymouth over the years has begun or ended its journey on the 'tramway and pier line' is impossible to estimate, but possibly the greater part. More readily assessed is benefit to the town. Although (discounting token wayleaves) the corporation has never received any direct payment in respect of the tramway, either for the line itself or 'per ton' or 'per passenger', indirect benefit has been substantial. Before the 1914 war, Great Western ships and their cargoes accounted for around 65 per cent of harbour revenue; additionally, perhaps half of the remaining 35 per cent accrued from other overseas traffic forwarded by rail. By the 1930s the proportion had risen to over 80 per cent, and after the 1939 war, through loss of other trade, over 90 per cent was attributable to traffic that, for a few years at least, continued to depend almost entirely on the tramway.

Nor should it be forgotten that successive harbour developments, from the 1870s to the 1970s, have been dictated entirely by the needs of the railway ships, and that without them, and the part played by the tramway, Weymouth as a commercial port would not exist today.

Plate 186: For enthusiasts' excursions to Wessex, inclusion of the trip to the quay has long been *de rigueur*. On 8th July 1979, the Great Western Society's train of GWR vehicles, having been down to the quay and back behind No. 33104, prepares to leave the 'up' loop behind Class 47 No. 47040.

MISCELLANY

Plate 187: A shunters' 'runner' had no part to play on the tramway and it was most unusual to see one there. On 30th April 1960 No. 7782 was switched from yard shunting at very short notice and did not wait to detach the runner.

Plate 188: The big 'snow-up' of early 1963 resulted in points at the quay, fitted with check rails, becoming clogged solid. An unconventional application of the steam lance provided an effective cure. This view was photographed on 3rd January 1963.

Plate 189 (Left): Wish you were here — something different for strolling holidaymakers to put on those cards home. The scene was photographed on 5th August 1963.

Plate 190: Another unfortunate mishap, this time on 24th August 1971. Because of the obstruction the boat train is entering the yard over the coal road.

Plate 191: In 1968 new-style carriage roof boards appeared, substituting 'train' for 'express' and adding the word 'quay'. The photograph was taken on 6th June 1968. These remained in use until 1978 — a very late survival — although latterly their use was somewhat sporadic.

Plates 192 (Below), 193 & 194 (Right): General Manager's inspections: (i) The saloon being propelled, near the Town Bridge, on 28th March 1961. (ii) The same train on Commercial Road, providing a good illustration of the use of lamps on the tramway. Under the chimney is the standard head lamp; on the drawhook is a red tail lamp, added for the return trip; and on the running plate one of the special Weymouth Quay lamps, spare, and a three-position hand lamp. Note also the driver's back, indicating the direction of travel. The engine was turned specially for the occasion. (iii) The modern equivalent, photographed at Ferry's Corner on 31st January 1984 (saloon No. TDB975025). Note the original 1865 alignment (centre foreground).

1368
JFX 73

Plates 195 & 196: A decision by the Association of British Travel Agents to hold their 1965 conference in Jersey resulted in a special sailing of the *Caesarea* with a sleeping car train in connection (23rd October). The train, consisting of ten Midland Region and Western Region cars and one ordinary carriage, ran through from Paddington — a rare occurrence since the boat trains were switched to Waterloo. In two other respects the working is thought to have been unique — sleeping cars on the tramway and a rostered double-heading by 'Drewries', because of the train's weight (about 450 tons). The train is shown (i) at the quay (in early morning mist!) and (ii) at Westham crossing, behind Nos. D2280 and D2295, on its return to the junction. Note the GBG plate on No. D2295, presumably shed by a visiting Guernsey car.

Plate 197: Inter-City Low Speed Train — the 'up' boat train consisting of Mk II stock behind No. 33042, on 2nd September 1984.

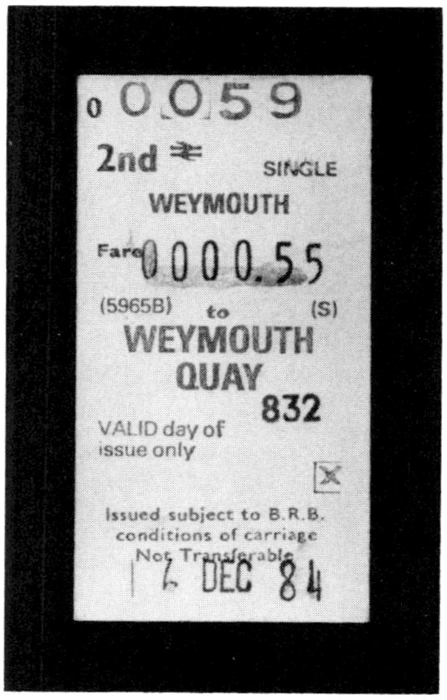

APPENDIX I

Abstract from the Appendix to the No. 3 Section of the Service Time Tables, May 1931.

Minor amendments to the following instructions, including a long-overdue deletion of the reference to shunting with horses, were incorporated in a re-issue dated December 1931 (Signal Notice S1444). The next revision, Notice S.2141, dated December 1947, was the last to be issued by the Great Western. Changes since then have necessitated more frequent updating, particularly during the last few years, since the end of 'traditional' tramway working. Despite such updating, substantial parts survive unchanged, an obvious case in point being the 4m.p.h. speed limit. Disregard of this was once not uncommon — e.g., *p.28* — and it would be idle to pretend that even in modern times, in the middle of the night, on an empty road, it has never been exceeded. There was, too, a classic case of 'bending the rules' one day in 1967, when a 'Drewry', its rendezvous with the boat train delayed by working at the quay, ran the length of the tramway in just eight minutes, escorted by a police car (par for the course about sixteen). On the other hand there are times when it is difficult to maintain 4m.p.h. and hearing a mother reprove her offspring 'come off the line — if the train was to come along you wouldn't stand a chance' one could only smile.

Other survivals can only be described as dead wood. For example, the maximum permitted axle loading shown in the current instructions (April 1984) is 16¾ tons (or tonnes) which relates to the 5700 class, long departed. Engines of Class 33 and the oil tank wagons — the latter now also departed — are specifically excepted, subject to a prohibition from working over sidings, but since there are no longer any effective sidings and the exceptions have, for practical purposes, made up the whole of the traffic since 1973, the effective limit may be regarded as 20 tons.

SHUNTING OPERATIONS AT WEYMOUTH JUNCTION IN CONNECTION WITH SPECIAL BOAT TRAIN, AND BOAT PORTION OF EXPRESS TRAIN OR OTHER PASSENGER TRAIN STARTING FROM THE UP PORTLAND LOOP LINE.

These Trains must in all cases be pushed, or otherwise placed, inside of the Starting Signal from Portland Branch to Up Main Line, and such Signal must not be lowered until the Trains have been so placed.

The Tram Engine when working a Passenger Train from the Quay must draw the whole of same in advance of the Points of the Scissors Crossing, and then back it in the direction of the Portland Branch sufficiently far to enable the Main Line Train Engine to back to it and stand inside of the Starting Signal.

SHUNTING OPERATIONS FROM TRAMWAY TO LOOP LINES AND VICE VERSA AT WEYMOUTH JUNCTION.

When it is necessary to make use of the Down Loop Line on the Portland Branch at Weymouth Junction for Shunting purposes to and from the direction of the Tramway, such operations must only be carried out under the following regulations :—

No Engine, with or without Trucks, must pass the Up Tramway Stop Signal, situated on the Goods Shed side of the Portland Branch Loop Lines and which controls Trains from the Tramway to the Up Loop Line, without the Shunter in charge of the Shunting operations being present, and without his verbal instructions as to what is required to be done.

Before the Shunter in charge of the Shunting operations orders a Shunt to be made past the Stop Signal in the direction of the Down Loop he must go, or telephone, to the Junction Signal Box, and, after making it clear to the Signalman there what he requires to do, obtain his permission to carry out the operation, and the Signalman must tell the person asking for such permission up to what point the Down Loop may be occupied.

Whenever practicable the Shunting operations must be performed over the Scissors Crossing to the Up Loop and the Up Tramway Signal lowered for this to be done.

After the Shunting operations have been completed, the person in charge of same must immediately inform the Signalman, and until he receives such advice nothing must be allowed to enter the Down Loop from either end.

No Engine, with or without Trucks, must be allowed to pass on to the Tramway until the Down Tramway Signal has been lowered, and it will be the duty of the Shunter in charge to inform the Signalman what is required, and the Shunter will be responsible for seeing the road is clear for the Shunting operations.

WORKING OF TRAMWAY GATES OPPOSITE GOODS SHED.

The above must be kept fastened when the Tramway Engine is not at work, and there are no trucks across the road.

When the work on the Tramway is finished, the Shunter in charge must see that the Gates are closed and fastened. If this cannot be done owing to trucks standing in the way, the Shunter who removes the trucks must at the same time close and fasten the Gates.

Care must be taken by all concerned when Shunting at this place to see that no damage is done to the Gates.

WEYMOUTH TRAMWAY AND PIER LINE.

1. The Tramway and Pier Line extends from the Junction with the Portland Line at Weymouth to the Landing Stage at the Pier.

2. There are various Sidings leading into the Tramway, and Catch Points have been fixed thereon to protect the Tramway Line. The Catch Points and Points leading into the Sidings are specially weighted, so that the normal position of the former shall be open, and the latter set for the proper running of Vehicles over the Tramway.

Weymouth—continued.

Weymouth Tramway and Pier Line—continued.

3. Loose levers are provided to work the Catch Points and Siding Points. The Head Shunter in charge is responsible for the custody of same, and he must have two in his possession when travelling with Trains over the Tramway.

4. The Engine for working Trains over the Tramway is provided with a bell and the Fireman is responsible for continuously ringing the same while the Train or Engine is in motion at any point between the Pier and the Goods Yard Entrance, at Weymouth Station.

5. Shunters employed on the Tramway Line must not couple or uncouple wagons in motion when shunting private sidings. In every case wagons must be brought to a stand before being coupled or uncoupled. **A special watch must be kept on the position of Mooring Rings, to ensure the Rings being kept clear of the Railway.**

6. **Passenger Trains.**—Great Western Passenger Trains will be worked between Weymouth Junction and the Weymouth Pier over the Tramway at times shewn in the Company's Working Time Tables from time to time, under the following Regulations :—

7. The Train must in every case be drawn by the Tramway Engine in both directions, and while running over the Tramway will be under the charge of the Weymouth Inspector on duty.

8. Before the Train is allowed to leave Weymouth Junction for the Pier, the duly-appointed Tramway Shunter in charge must take the Tram Engine over the Tramway, and see that all Trucks are placed inside of the Catch Points, and that all Points are properly set for the safe running of the Train, and he must, before the Train leaves the Weymouth Junction, report to the Inspector in charge of the Train that such has been done.

9. When the Train is ready to leave for the Pier, the Tramway Pilotman, on being instructed by the Inspector in charge to do so, must walk between 30 and 50 yards (according to gradients and curves) in front of the Passenger Train to the Pier, and see that the Line is perfectly clear for the passage of the Train, and warn every person on or about the Tramway of the approach of the Train, by means of blowing a Guard's whistle, with which he is supplied, and he must also see that the Train does not exceed a speed of 4 miles an hour.

10. The same course must be adopted before a Train is allowed to leave the Pier for Weymouth Junction, that is, the Tramway Pilotman must, before the Train is allowed to start, take the Train Engine over the Tramway, and see that all Trucks are placed inside of the Catch Points, andthat all Points are properly set for the safe running of the Train. The Train must not be started by the Inspector in charge of the Train until he has been satisfied by the Tramway Pilotman that the Line is clear. The Pilotman must then walk between 30 and 50 yards (according to gradients and curves) in front of Train, and carry out the instructions as laid down in Clause 9.

11. In consequence of the sharp curves, Passenger Trains must not be coupled up with the ordinary couplings, which must be taken off and hung on the hook under the carriage. Loose couplings, specially provided, must be used for each Vehicle, so as to give perfect freedom in running round curves, and the vacuum pipes must be connected up on each Vehicle so that the vacuum connection shall be complete from the Engine to the last Vehicle conveying Passengers, and it will be the duty of the Inspector to see that this is done before the Train starts from either end.

With the excepton of the "articulated" Trains, Passenger Vehicles worked over this Section must not exceed 9 feet $3\frac{1}{4}$ inches wide over projections and 59 feet 4 inches in length or a distance ("centre to centre" of bogies) of more than 42 feet, or with an overhang from centre of bogie to the buffer of more than 10 feet. (A certain number of 60 feet vehicles are authorised to work over this section, and a list giving the registered numbers of these is available.)

Passenger Train Vehicles of the corridor class worked over the Tramway must have all the Gangways and Hoods properly disconnected, and the doors secured (after which the screw couplings are to be slackened out and taken off for the loose couplings to be put on) before the Train leaves Weymouth Junction.

The Station dispatching a Train formed with Coaches or Vans of this description, or if worked from a Foreign Line, the last stopping Station before reaching Yeovil, must wire the Weymouth Station Master to arrange suitable Staff to perform the work of uncoupling.

Coaching Stock with close-buffers and connections must not be attached to a Train for Weymouth Quay under any circumstances.

Passenger Train Working to Cargo Stage.—When it is necessary to work the Passenger Train to the Cargo Stage, the points leading into the Cargo Stage Road must be securely wedged and the lever working the points must be firmly held by the Pilotman while the whole of the Train passes into the Siding. Similar arrangements must be made when the Passenger Train is started from the Siding.

12. The usual Head and Tail Signals must be used with all Trains, Passenger and Goods and Light Engines running over the Tramway. Side Lamps must also be carried on Passenger Trains.

13. **Goods Traffic.**—The working of Goods Traffic will be regulated according to the requirements of the Great Western and S.R. Companies respectively. The Engine appointed for the work will be under the immediate control of the Shunter on duty, who has charge of the work on the Tramway, and who will be responsible for all regulations with regard to the working of the Engine being strictly carried out. The person in charge will be responsible for seeing that the traffic along and upon the Tramway is properly and efficiently accommodated without preference. The convenience of Traders in loading and unloading Trucks at the Stores upon the Tramway must also be studied.

14. The Engine must always be accompanied by a Shunter who will be responsible for seeing that the road is clear in front of the Engine, and who must warn everyone on or about the Tramway of the Engine's approach, and must also see that the Engine does not travel faster than the specified speed (4 miles per hour). He must either walk 30 to 50 yards in front of the Train, or ride on the front buffer-plank of the Engine (except for a distance of 50 yards either side of the Town Bridge, which ground must be covered on foot),

Weymouth—continued.

Weymouth Tramway and Pier Line—continued.

but if there is a Vehicle being pushed in front of the Engine, he must walk in front of the same. When the load of a Train from Weymouth Quay consists of 30 wagons or more the Weymouth Quay Traffic Agent will provide a second man for the purpose of giving whatever warning is necessary to ensure the Line being kept clear for an approaching Train ; this man must walk 100 yards in front of the Train. Vehicles must not be pushed over any portion of the Tramway except for shunting or other purposes, unless absolutely necessary.

The load must not exceed 45 4-wheel wagons or equivalent thereto.

15. **Level Crossing leading to Westham Bridge.**—EVERY TRAIN (Passenger and Goods) must STOP DEAD before reaching the Crossing leading to the Westham Bridge as follows :—

Down Trains.—50 yards on the Station side of the Crossing ;

Up Trains.—50 yards on the Pier side of the Crossing ;

and must not proceed in the direction of the Crossing until the Tramway Pilotman has reached the Crossing and given an " All Right " Signal from there for the Train to proceed.

16. **Melcombe Regis Station Approach Road.**—The Approach Road to Melcombe Regis Station crosses the Tramway, and Drivers and Pilotmen in charge of Trains and Engines must exercise great caution when approaching this road in either direction.

17. During the time Melcombe Regis Station is open for traffic, all Trains and Engines must come to a stand before crossing the Approach Road, and must not proceed until an " All Right " Signal has been given by the Pilotman in charge, who is responsible for seeing that the Approach Road is clear and that the public is properly warned.

18. **Great Western Engines Working Special Trains from the Tramway.**—When necessary through Trains from the Tramway Line must be brought to a stand clear of and on the Quay side of the Approach Road to Melcombe Regis Station, at which point the Train Engine may be attached. The Train Engine, however, must not be taken beyond the corner of the Gardens.

19. **General Instructions.**—In going round sharp curves and when passing openings of Streets, and at those places where there are many children on or about the Tramway, the Pilotman must always walk 30 to 50 yards ahead of the Engine, so as to be able to warn people of its approach, and to keep the road clear. Where the road is straight and there are no people about, he may ride upon the Engine, except with Passenger Trains, before which he must walk the whole distance.

He must be provided with a Guard's whistle, and a set of flags by day, and a Guard's Hand Lamp by night.

20. The Line on each side of the Town Bridge is on a rising gradient. With Trains consisting of heavy loads, it may be necessary to exceed the speed of 4 miles per hour, when running under the Bridge, to enable them to reach the summit. Drivers of such Trains must exercise the greatest possible care in running up the gradient and round the curve on the Station side of the Bridge, and they must only attain such a speed as will enable them to take their Trains to the top and to stop clear of any obstruction.

21. The speed of the Train or Engine must not exceed 4 miles an hour, except as shewn above, and it must travel slower where it is necessary to ensure safety.

In case of its being necessary, by day, to leave trucks standing on the Tramway Line at or near the top of the Incline, on the Station side of the Town Bridge, such Vehicles must be secured by the hand brakes being tightly fastened down by a sprag placed in the leading wheels of Vehicle nearest the Pier. After dark the Tramway Line must not be fouled.

22. When the Train is stopped under any circumstances, the Shunter in charge of Engine and the Pilotman must look along both sides of the Line, to see that all is right, before a signal to start is given.

23. The greatest care and vigilance must be exercised by each person accompanying the Train or Engine to guard against accident, and ensure the safety of the public ; and the Engine Driver must implicitly obey any signal or instruction given by the Tramway Pilotman, or Shunter.

A Portable Crane is stationed at the end of the Mileage Siding, West End of Cargo Stage, and when the Crane is not in use the extension girders must be placed clear of the Tramway and Siding connection, and jib secured in this position.

The Tramway Pilotman will be held responsible for seeing that this has been done before allowing vehicles to pass this point in either direction. The dead end Points at this end of the Siding to be normally secured leading to Tramway, but to be reversed for the passage of Passenger Trains.

Marine Coal Siding.—Under no circumstances must Empty Coal or other Wagons be pushed out foul of the Running Line unless the authorised Tramway Pilotman or Coal Foreman is present to work the points and arrange clearance of the Vehicles from the Tramway.

Bagg's Siding, Couzen's Siding.—Special care must be exercised in moving wagons into or out of either of these Sidings. The Pilotman must walk between 30 and 50 yards ahead of the trucks for the purpose of issuing any warning that may be necessary. The Shunter to operate the hand points.

The regulations apply to Light Engines as well as Trains, and they must be scrupulously observed by all concerned.

WORKING TWO ENGINES ON THE TRAMWAY AT ONE TIME.

1. To facilitate the working of the Tramway, two Engines may be worked between the Pier and Weymouth Goods Yard under the following special regulations :—

2. Each Engine will be under the charge of a Tramway Pilotman ; a Shunter will also work with each Engine and an Inspector will supervise in all cases of Passenger Train working, and an Inspector or Foreman in cases of Goods Train working.

3. Each Engine must be equipped with a Bell, which must be rung in accordance with the General Regulations for working the Tramway referred to above.

Weymouth—continued.

Working two Engines on the Tramway at one time—continued.

4. The person responsible for the working of the Tramway must supervise the working generally, and under no circumstances must he allow two Engines at the same time to be on the Tramway between the Station and the Caution Board, fixed opposite Nicholas Street, situated about 120 yards on the Station side of the Town Bridge. Before the second Engine proceeds beyond the Caution Board towards the Pier, the Shunter who accompanies the second Engine must get permission from the person in charge, and must come to a clear understanding as to what is required to be done, and take all necessary precautions to ensure safety.

5. **Working of Passenger Trains.**—The Tramway must be cleared of all Trucks and other obstructions for the passage of the Boat Train over the Tramway, and the Engine appointed to clear the Tramway must, immediately after it has done so, be placed in one of the Loops or Sidings, under the personal supervision of the person in charge of Tramway, and under no circumstances must it be removed from that position without his personal and verbal instructions.

6. The Boat Train must not under any circumstances pass the Caution Board fixed opposite Nicholas Street, situated about 120 yards on the Station side of the Town Bridge, without the permission of the person in charge of Tramway who must, after placing the Light Engine in the Loop or Siding, proceed to the Caution Board and personally pilot the Boat Train from there past the Loop or Siding where the Light Engine has been placed.

7. After the departure of the Boat Train from the Pier, the Light Engine must at once replace the Trucks, as required on the Tramway, and afterwards work between the Pier and Station according to requirements, either with trucks or light.

Provided always that when one Engine is on the Quay side of the Caution Board the other Engine must stop at the Caution Board until the Shunter accompanying the Engine on the Station side has obtained permission from the person in charge of Tramway to proceed in the direction of the Cargo Stage.

The Inspector in charge of the Quay working will give all necessary instructions to the person in charge of the Tramway.

WORKING OF PASSENGER TRAINS, LIGHT ENGINES, GOODS TRUCKS, ETC., OVER THE TRAMWAY AT THE TOWN BRIDGE

1. Except in broad daylight all Down Passenger Trains, empty Coach Trains, and Engines with or without trucks, must be brought to a dead stand at a point about 50 yards on the Station side of the Town Bridge, and in like manner Up Trains and Engines, with or without trucks, must be brought to a dead stand at a point about 50 yards on the Pier side of the Town Bridge.

2. The Pilotman whose duty it is to precede Trains and Engines when running over the Tramway, must, after such Trains have been brought to a stand, proceed to the Town Bridge, and satisfy himself that the lines under the Bridge and the approaches thereto are absolutely clear for Trains or Engines with or without trucks to come forward, and the Driver of same must not proceed towards the Bridge until he receives verbal authority from the Pilotman to do so.

3. In broad daylight, Trains and Engines, with or without trucks, must be worked in accordance with the regulations set forth in this Appendix. The Pilotman appointed to work with such Trains must, however, be careful to see that no person is on the Tramway under the Bridge, and that no obstruction exists there, and in the event of anything in the nature of an obstruction being observed, he must take steps to stop the Train or Engine, as the case may be.

REGULATIONS FOR SHUNTING OPERATIONS WHILE PASSENGER STEAMERS ARE BERTHED AT THE CARGO STAGE.

During the time the Passenger Steamers are berthed at the Cargo Stage at Weymouth, and from 8.30 p.m. till the Steamer leaves the Cargo Stage for the Pier when Passengers for the Channel Islands are allowed to go on board, shunting operations with the Tram Engine, or with horses, must be carried on with the greatest care, and under the following regulations :—

Before any Vehicle is moved in the direction of the Cargo Stage, whether from the direction of the Pier or from the direction of the Town Bridge, either by Engine or by horses, the Shunter in charge of the operation is held responsible for personally seeing that no Passenger or other person, except the Company's servants, is allowed to cross the Tramway at the end towards which the Vehicles are being moved, either to go to the Stage or from it, until such shunting operations have been carried out, or the Vehicles are at a complete rest, and the passage across the Tramway to or from the Cargo Stage is properly protected, either by verbally instructing the Driver of the Engine or horses, or by exhibiting a Danger Signal (red flag by day and red light by night).

As a rule passengers will join the Steamer at the Cargo Stage by means of movable steps placed across the Cargo Stage Tramway line, and these must be placed in position, for that purpose only, by the Foreman in charge of the Cargo Stage for the time being, who must, before doing so, place a red light by night, or red flag by day, on the end of the Vehicle nearest to the Town Bridge, in such a position as to be clearly seen by the Driver of an approaching Engine and by the Shunter in charge of same or of trucks being shunted by horses ; and a similar Signal on the post erected at the Town Bridge end of the Stage. A red lamp must also be affixed to the end of the Vehicle nearest to the Pier. Such Signals must be kept so exhibited

Weymouth—continued.

Regulations for Shunting Operations while Passenger Steamers are berthed at the Cargo Stage—continued.

during the whole time the steps are foul of the Line, and the Foreman in charge must personally see that no Vehicles are moved in the direction of the steps whilst so placed. The Foreman must also verbally instruct the person performing the shunting operations, both by Engines and horses, that the Line is occupied by the steps.

If there are no Trucks on the Tramway Line when the steps are placed there, the Danger Signal (red light by night and red flag by day) must be exhibited from the Signal Post at the Town Bridge end of the Stage.

The Inspector in charge of the Stage for the time being is the sole person authorised to remove the Danger Signal as specified in the preceding clauses. He must not do so until he has caused the steps to be removed.

To avoid risk of accident one loud whistle will be given by the Quay Inspector in charge of the work at the stage when Vehicles are about to be moved and no person must then be allowed to cross the buffers of Wagons, cross over the Wagons, or underneath them.

The employees are reminded that in all cases it is advisable to pass between the Road and Cargo Stage or vice versa by the steps provided for the purpose at either end of the Cargo Stage.

ADDITIONAL INSTRUCTIONS FOR THE WORKING OF PASSENGER TRAINS OVER THE TRAMWAY.

Engines of a special class are provided for working over the Tramway between Weymouth Junction and the Pier.

Passenger Trains over the Tramway must not exceed one engine load, viz., 96 wheels.

Down Boat Trains.			**Instructions re working over Tramway.**
The following advices must be sent.			
By	To	Stating	
	Day Boat Trains.		When necessary to divide Train to be done at Weymouth Junction (exception in clause *d*), both portions being worked as per Tramway instructions, plus :— (a) The work must be supervised by an Inspector. (b) The coaches of the first part must, after being unloaded, be put away into the Cargo Stage Road or other Siding and be properly secured in same, and the Driver must be instructed not to move his Engine until the second portion has passed and cleared the point where the first portion stands. (c) Second part by day not to follow first part with less than 5 minutes interval, and 15 minutes interval by night. Second part day Train not to proceed beyond Stop board fixed opposite Nicholas Street, and in case of second part of night Train it must come to a stand opposite Bagg's Timber yard (passengers must be prevented from alighting here) in each case to await arrival of Inspector or person in charge of Tramway to pilot it to the Pier. (d) In case a division has to be made with either a day or night boat Train when there is only one Engine on the Tramway, such division must be arranged after the Boat Train has been brought to a stand opposite Bagg's Timber Yard (passengers must not be allowed to get out of Train here), and the precautions mentioned in foregoing paragraphs must be observed.
Westbury	Weymouth Town .. ,, Quay ..	Number of passengers and wheels for the Quay on Train when leaving Westbury.	
Yeovil	Weymouth Town .. ,, Quay ..	When Train added to or reduced there.	
Paddington ..	Westbury .. .. Weymouth Town .. ,, Quay ..	When load exceeds 56 wheels.	
	Night Boat Trains.		
Swindon	Weymouth Town .. ,, Quay ..	When load exceeds 72 wheels.	
Westbury	Weymouth Town .. ,, Quay ..	Number of wheels on Train.	

APPENDIX II

Particulars of tramway duties, extracted from the Weymouth station master's register c.1890 *et seq*:

Assistant Inspector E.H. Price
hours of duty 2p.m. – 2.45a.m. or as soon as work is finished; tea 4.25 till 8.0
General duties: On duty to meet Boat and count passengers at 2p.m., also check and collect Tickets from passengers on landing, assists in seeing passengers in train, Luggage stowed and parcels loaded correctly, giving this assistance to Guard of Train, who takes charge of train at Portland Junction No. 1 Box.

See coaches are in clean condition and examine all Tickets after Passengers in train, taking a register of same, also sees loose couplings are on train for safety in running up Tram, starts train after getting all right from Clerk in Charge at Quay, on arrival at Junction sees all couplings are closely connected up, Vacuum all in order and Roping in proper condition, and lamps supplied where necessary, also that Footwarmers are placed in each compartment at Quay during Winter.

After departure of train at 4.15p.m. or later goes to his Tea until 8p.m.

On duty passenger platform at 8.00p.m. and in charge of station and staff until arrival of Boat Train which he meets at Junction dividing same and sending one portion into station, the remaining or quay portion he accompanies down Tram seeing that loose couplings are brought into use before this portion leaves Junction, on arrival at Quay sees train cleared and with Tram Engine puts Train in order for next days working leaving coaches at quay.

He leaves in Inspectors Office at Station a list of coaches at quay showing what accommodation there is of the different classes also furnishing the information of counting from Boat, No. of passengers in different classes in up Boat Train and other matters to Station Master, also hands in daily a statement shewing number of passengers in Boat Train for Steamer and Town. Keeps record of Parcels sent down by Boat Train over Tramway.

J. Travers Goods Inspector, Tramway
hours of duty, start 10a.m., finish weekdays after the traffic is put on train, after delivery of the fish off last down train to the boat.

This man is responsible for the general working of the tramway under the direction of the Quay Inspector, he is to shunt and regulate the traffic between the station and the Boats. Channel Islands — special potatoes, and private freighters as the case may be, both up and down.

He will similarly deal with the ship's coal and heavy stores, put out empties at the various warehouses and depots for the use of the traders along the Tramway and line of Quay as required daily or nightly. He will also deal with the South Western Company's traffic at the Quay, and over the Tramway in the same way, and giving them equal attention with ourselves.

The Train Engine to bring the wagons up as far as practicable in station order to save time.

The Tram Inspector to act as a communication between the Quay and the station — taking his instructions from the Quay Inspector and to keep the Station Foreman or shunter advised of the progress of the trucking etc. at the Quay — probable loads to come up, and time to be expected — what traffic is required to be put out, and time and order.

In cases of emergency or necessity to alter the working arrangements, the telegraph between the Quay and the station to be used. Responsible for seeing that the special printed (or other) regulations for working the Tramway are strictly carried out. See Instructions dated July 1889.

Vowles, G Tramway Flagman
hours of duty 2.0p.m. to 2.45a.m. or as soon as engine has come back from the pier. Meals are taken between trips up and down the Tramway as time will allow, time not to exceed two and a half hours.
Duties etc. To accompany Tram Engine to and from the Station on every trip and walk before it exhibiting the necessary signals and taking other precautions to ensure safety as laid down in the Instructions for working the Tramway dated July 1889. To perform shunting operations as may be necessary on Tramway and at Quay.

Note: Like the engine roster detailed on *page 29* the hours of duty for the appointed tramway staff were governed by the steamer times. They applied also to the appointed staff at the quay. Inspector Travers's hours were later altered to bring them into line (2p.m. to 1.30a.m.). The potato traffic in season and, after 1897, the summer passenger sailings, must have involved additional attendance, but no details are available.

About 1899 Price was promoted to inspector and John Gill, the station inspector, became responsible for the tramway:

Tramway Inspector Gill
hours of duty 9.0a.m. to 9.0p.m. subject to alteration to meet requirements; one hour dinner, one hour tea

To regulate the working of the Tramway with the object of giving the best possible service to traffic and to the Company's ships and also to the Merchants' etc. traffic.

To be in touch with the Marine Department by Telephone or otherwise and see that traffic from and to the Steamers is worked in accordance with the requirements of the Marine Department, regard being had to the other requirements affecting the working of the Goods Yard.

When the hours of working on the Tramway are unusual he must arrange the duties of the Tramway Inspector and Pilotman in conjunction with the Station Inspector. To keep an eye upon the quantity of traffic standing here and at the Loco Sidings awaiting shipment and when it is excessive call the special attention of the Station Master to it. He must see that Goods traffic is sent down for Shipment in preference to Potato empties and that in all cases the oldest wagons are sent down first.

If any traffic is kept here unduly awaiting Shipment, he must call the Stationmaster's attention to it.

To see the dispatch of fruit traffic from the Station whenever possible and always before leaving duty see that the proper arrangements are made for dealing with it, and special trains arranged if such are required.

To supervise as far as possible the whole working over the Tramway and see that it is properly performed and the rules as shown in Appendix No. 2 carried out.

To attend to the requirements of the Merchants and Traders along the Tramway visiting their offices from time to time and canvassing for their traffic. Take up and deal with any complaint from the Traders as to Tramway Working, and take measures to avoid these complaints as far as possible.

See that grain and other traffic loaded on the Tramway for G.W. line is loaded, checked, sheeted and labelled properly, by the persons appointed for these duties. As far as possible see that this traffic is duly consigned and the consignment notes promptly sent up to the Station.

To keep the Station advised as far as possible of the requirements on the Tramway and at the Quay.

To supervise the Tramway men and see that they perform their duties properly. Inspector Travers is not relieved of any of the duties hitherto performed by him. See that wagons are not delayed unduly under load on the Tramway, seeing the consignees if necessary, and pressing them to discharge the wagons.

To satisfy himself from time to time that signatures for Goods sent down the Tramway are duly obtained. When a shunting horse is employed on the Tramway, see that this is really necessary and record the dates and times the horse is so employed.

To render any assistance he can in the Goods Yard, particularly in the Potato & Fruit Seasons, and when possible see to the dispatch of the Fruit Specials and 7.20 London Goods.

In the Potato Season to give special attention to this traffic and watch the supply of empty wagons available for the traffic.

When a day Boat is running, see that the Tramway is cleared in good time for the Boat Train.

and, as though looking after the tramway were not enough –

To canvas (sic) for Naval and Military Traffic at Portland and Weymouth when required. Take opportunities of inspecting Time Tables and Time Bills in the Town, also the Billposting Stations to see that a good show of this Company's Bills is made.

To be at the disposal of the Station Master for other duties as may be required from time to time.

APPENDIX III

Tramway Sidings etc. List of Agreements

Location	*Agreement Date*	*Parties to Agreement*	*Wayleave or Rent*	*Notes*
Ferry's Corner				
'Causeway'	8-5-1867	Cpn, W&PR	—	Out of use c.1963. Abandoned 1984
Widening	19-3-1938	Cpn, W&PR, GWR, SR	—	
	1-7-1938	Cpn, GWR	—	
Farthing's siding	before 1880	Cpn, GWR	—	Lifted 1939
Cargo stage loop	10-4-1880	Cpn, GWR	—	Now through road to pier
Coal road	24-10-1881	Cpn, GWR	5/- p.a.	Lifted 1974
Templeman's siding	27-5-1882	Cpn, GWR	5/- p.a.	Agreement terminated 1948
	22-12-1954	Cpn, BTC	5/- p.a.	Out of use since 1972 †
Bagg's siding	c.1882	Cpn, GWR, LSWR (?)	10/- p.a.	*‡Tarred over 1978
Cosens's siding	10-6-1884	Cpn, GWR, LSWR	5/- p.a.	*Lifted 1957
George loop	16-4-1885	Cpn, GWR, LSWR	5/- p.a.	
Passenger landing stage	15-8-1888	Cpn, GWR	5/- p.a.	Incorporated into new pier, 1933/4
Marine coal siding	5-4-1899	GWR, Mr. Jno Bagg	£20 p.a.	Opened 1904. Out of use circa 1947
Melcome Regis siding	30-3-1916	Cpn, GWR	5/- p.a.	Laid in 1915 for wartime traffic. Lifted 1974
Pier reconstruction	31-12-1930	Cpn, GWR	—	} Pier roads shortened 1972
	20-2-1961	Cpn, BTC	—	
Backwater sidings	20-2-1961	Cpn, BTC	—	Lifted 1972

†*End of freight traffic; last recorded use, 1969.*
* *Previously laid as temporary siding.* ‡*Formerly Greenwood's siding.*
(Greenwood's Steam Saw Mills bankrupt November 1883); later Webb Major's siding.

APPENDIX IV

Miscellany

Tramway Tolls

The Town Clerk read a letter from the Great Western Railway Co. in which they stated that they had made reduced rates for the carriage of grain and oilcake and that arrangements had also been made to reduce the tramway charges from 8d. to 6d. per ton.

Report of Council Meeting, 14th April 1886

On and from January 1st 1896 the charge for conveyance of Grain traffic over the Weymouth Tramway will be as follows:

(1) 3d. per ton for loads of 4 tons and upwards
(2) 4d. per ton for loads between 2 and 4 tons
(3) 6d. per ton for less lots than 2 tons

Proportioned as follows

Haulage to G.W.R.	*Payment to Joint Line*
(1) 2d.	1d.
(2) 2d.	2d.
(3) 3d.	3d.

6.8.98 Agreed by Mr Maiden* and L. & S.W. Co. that in dealing with future settlements of the Joint Account charges shall be made as under for Live stock passing over the Tramway.

	charge	*Haulage to G.W.R.*	*Payment to Joint Line*
Live stock per Truck	1/6	9d.	9d.
Live stock per part Truck	1/-	6d.	6d.

General Traffic
6d. per ton, minimum charge as for 3 tons per truck.

* *G.W.R. Chief Goods Manager*

Grain and oilcake were both prominent among traffics conveyed over the tramway but not subject to through rates. The apportionment is interesting. The last two items are from the Weymouth station register.

The Weymouth Town Council decided at their meeting on the 8th Feb 1893 to charge the Company 5/- per annum for Water used at the Pier for the purpose of washing carriages and Mr Lambert agreed to pay this amount as from Jany 1. 1893.

Item in Weymouth station register, 20th Feb 1893

Chas. Jolliffe, carrier, was summoned under the Towns Police Act for allowing trucks . . . to remain . . . on a siding . . . longer than necessary, to the inconvenience of the public. Case dismissed.
News item, *Dorset County Chronicle*, 22nd November 1877

. . . the Companies have statutory authority to run their trains along the Tramway at the point in question & Mr Templeman has no right to complain of any such user but care should be taken that no unnecessary obstruction is caused by standing trucks upon it so as to interfere more than is avoidable with Mr Templeman's right to use what is after all a Public Street.

R.R. Nelson, G.W.R. Solicitor, to J.L. Wilkinson, General Manager, 11th April 1902

Dear Sir

Coal truck pushed foul of the Tramway Weymouth

I send you a copy of an extract of a letter received from our Solicitors in regard to the working of the tramway . . .

I have told our London people that we have always endeavoured to work in harmony with all the freighters & to subject them to the least possible annoyance or inconvenience in connection with the working of our very heavy traffic over the Tramway and that this shall continue to be done. On the other hand we must insist on the freighters bending to our requirements and if any case of obstruction occurs please report the facts specially to me.

Letter from the Divisional Superintendent, Bristol, to Weymouth station master, 19th April 1902

Weymouth Magistrates dealt with 15 summonses against people who had parked vehicles on the Quay, obstructing the boat trains.

All the defendants were fined £25 each, and ordered to pay costs of £24.38.

News Item, *Dorset Evening Echo*, 27th July 1983.

INDEX

Page numbers in italics relate to illustrations

INDEX